Tim Duffy

MICROSOFT® Windows 95®

ADDISON-WESLEY

An imprint of Addison Wesley Longman, Inc.

Reading, Massachusetts ▲ Menlo Park, California ▲ New York
Harlow, England ▲ Don Mills, Ontario ▲ Sydney ▲ Mexico City ▲ Madrid ▲ Amsterdam

Senior Editor: *Carol Crowell*
Project Manager: *Bess Deck*
Senior Production Supervisor: *Juliet Silveri*
Production Services: *Sue Purdy Pelosi*
Copyeditor: *Barbara Conway*
Proofreader: *Holly McLean-Aldis*
Technical Editor: *Dawn Remmel*
Indexers: *Mark Kmetzco, Bernice Eisen*
Page Checking: *MaryBeth Pitman, Cynthia Benn*
Compositor: *Compset Inc.*
Technical Art Consultant: *Joe Vetere*
Cover Design Supervisor: *Gina Hagen*
Text and cover design: *Linda Wade*
Marketing Manager: *Michelle Hudson*
Manufacturing Manager: *Hugh Crawford*

ISBN 0-201-31517-3

Addison-Wesley Publishing Company
Jacob Way
Reading, MA 01867
Web: http://www.awl.com/he/is/
Email: is@aw.com

1 2 3 4 5 6 7 8 9 10-DOW-00999897

To Wendy and Michael,
The two most important people in my life

PREFACE

Computer literacy is becoming a necessity in a world supercharged with information that is constantly evolving and updating. Millions of computers, both individually and in vast networks that span the globe, are constantly processing, analyzing, and organizing information. Advances in hardware and technology that once took decades, then years, now occur with startling frequency.

The challenge is real, it is identifiable, and it is immediate. What does one need to know to achieve and maintain both academic and business success in this technological maelstrom? For more than two decades, a professor at Illinois State University has been answering this question. His name is Tim Duffy, and he is both a teacher and a writer. As a teacher, he has taught introductory computer courses to thousands of his own students; as an author, he has introduced the very same computing concepts and skills to millions of students worldwide through his highly successful series.

In both his classes and his books, Duffy achieves a perfect balance between concept and skill, the why and the how, of computing. The why is the foundation of computing. Learn the concept and why that concept is important, and you can implement any skill. Because he teaches introductory computing throughout the school year, Duffy has intimate knowledge of exactly what conceptual information and what techniques students need and want to learn, and how to present enough of each to interest and challenge these active learners. Duffy knows what works in the classroom and what works in the computer labs. He knows where students can trip up, what assignments will make them think, what examples and exercises will illuminate the concepts, and what techniques will teach.

Duffy teaches what he writes and writes what he teaches. In his books, he brings his classroom teaching experience directly to you with the most innovative, up-to-date material available anywhere. His pedagogy is classroom tried and tested. There are completely new exercises and assignments, an all-new Windows 95-influenced design, and eye-popping graphics for today's visually oriented students. There are Internet and World Wide Web examples and active learning projects. The new Running Case sections are built around everyday problems that require both critical thinking and mastery of specific skills.

BUILDING KNOWLEDGE

For Duffy, learning is like building knowledge. A concept is presented, a feature or task is briefly described, and then students work with it. They complete an exercise or practice a task. Once that task is learned, they add a little more, building on what they are learning. After completing a small group of such tasks, each within its own context, students are presented with projects that unify the concepts and the skills. To achieve this natural balance between concepts and skills, there is constant reinforcement and evaluation throughout the book, including:

- **Active Learning.** Exercises apply software commands and features of each Office 97 application program to a specific problem, reinforcing skills described in the text.
- **Running Cases.** Everyday problems are presented with just enough information to challenge the students. The Running Case teaches critical thinking while reinforcing the basic skills that students have learned to that point.
- **Document to Web Presentation.** In-depth coverage shows students how to turn an ordinary document into a professional presentation, enhance its appearance, put it on the Web, and then improve the Web page to produce a professional electronic document.
- **Task Steps and Reference.** Reinforcing the Exercise sections provide students with summary information on how a task is performed to reinforce learning and to provide a reference for the future.
- **Self-Learning.** On Your Own boxes allow students to gain additional mastery of features as they explore Office 97 applications on their own.
- **Timely Tips.** Special notations tell students what potential traps they may encounter with a software tool, what can go wrong, and how to remedy the problem.
- **Toolbar Button Reference.** Tables of toolbar buttons give students a central location to find summaries of buttons found on frequently used toolbars.
- **Keyboard and Toolbar Icons.** Task-specific icons appear frequently in headings and tables to help students identify and remember keystrokes or toolbar buttons.
- **Self-Evaluation.** End-of-session exercises offer reinforcement in multiple formats: true/false, multiple choice, short answer, and project-based questions.
- **Unifying Features.** In *Office 97 Professional,* common features of Office 97 applications are covered first to give students the big picture of how to use an integrated suite.

Save Command File, Save or [Save]

The Save command allows you to immediately save the active document. You may use the Save command periodically to save any changes that you have made in a document. You are generally encouraged to use some version of the Save command every 10 to 15 minutes or so to save your work to disk. Then, if the power goes out, all that you will have to redo is the work you've done since the last Save command.

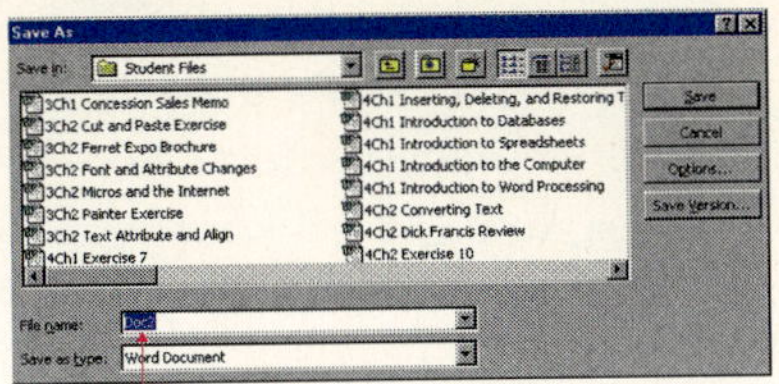

Figure 1.31
Using the Save As dialog box, you can save a document for the first time, change the name of a document, or store a document in a different location on the disk.

Providing Web Access to a File

Office applications permit you to save just about any document as an HTML file using the command sequence File, Save as HTML. It invokes the Save As HTML dialog box shown in Figure 1.33.

This feature allows you to create a document that you can retrieve directly using Internet Explorer. You can save a file as an HTML document on your local disk, or you can specify a URL to which you want the document saved.

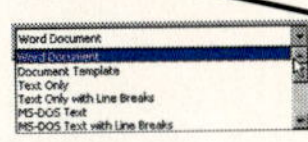

Figure 1.32
The available formats that Word can use to save a file to disk.

TIMELY TIP

Office has a built-in automatic save feature that you can use to restore some of your lost work. This AutoSave feature saves every 10 minutes or so. If you restart your computer after a power outage and then start the software application that you were using when you lost power, you will be stepped through the procedure of recovering the data. However you can recover only the data entered prior to the last AutoSave operation.

This feature can be activated by issuing the Tool, Options command sequence. When the Options dialog box opens, click the Save tab and examine the AutoRecover portion of the tab.

Duffy takes advantage of the **Web-aware tools** provided with Office 97 to help students translate their skills for use with the Internet and the Web.

Timely Tips inform students of helpful shortcuts, potential mistakes, or troubleshooting measures they can use with the text.

graphic included in that box varies depending on the type of Office Assistant you choose. Figure 1.4 shows the default Office Assistant called Clippit.

Usually, the Office Assistant feature is activated when you start any Office Application. If it does not appear on your screen, you can activate it by clicking the Office Assistant button on the toolbar. Initially the Office Assistant appears something like Clippit shown in Figure 1.4. The appearance of the box changes, however, as you perform tasks within that application.

If you perform a task that the Office Assistant thinks can be done more efficiently, it offers help without waiting for you to ask. A light bulb appears in the upper-right corner of the Office Assistant box (Figure 1.5). The appearance of the graphic changes, and a bubble displays a brief statement about the task you just performed. When you click an Office Assistant box with this appearance, the Office Assistant provides additional information on how you can make the task easier (Figure 1.6).

If you run into a problem and want the Office Assistant to help you, you can click the Office Assistant box to get its attention. The Office Assistant should look like that shown in Figure 1.7. If, for example, you want information about printing, you type the word *printing* in the box and then click the Search button. A list of topics appears, as shown in Figure 1.8. You can click on any topic to receive further information.

Information about the Print a document option appears in Figure 1.9. As you can see, this option generates a list of printing-related topics. Choosing the Print a range of pages option results in the Help screen shown in Figure 1.10.

You can change the type of Office Assistant from the default of Clippit to one of about eight other versions Office provides. When you right-click on the Office Assistant box, a context menu appears. Click the Options menu item to open the Office Assistant dialog box. Click the Gallery tab, and your screen should appear similar to the one shown in Figure 1.11. Follow the instructions given in the dialog box to examine the various Office Assistants and make your selection.

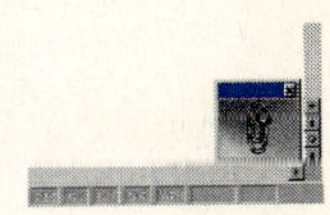

Figure 1.4
Clippit, the default Office Assistant.

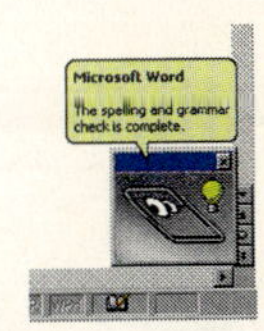

Figure 1.5
The Office Assistant offering to help you with the task of checking spelling.

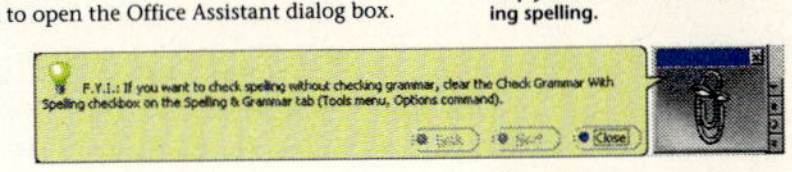

Figure 1.6
Additional information provided by the Office Assistant on using Word's spelling checker efficiently.

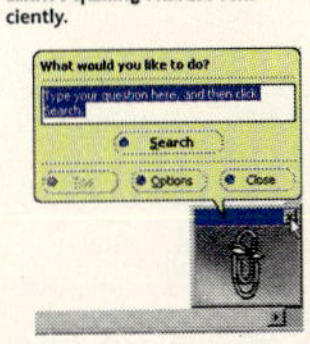

Figure 1.7
The Office Assistant ready to help you.

TIMELY TIP

If you have a sound system hooked to your computer, you can hear the Office Assistant making various sounds as you enter an Office document or perform tasks on a document.

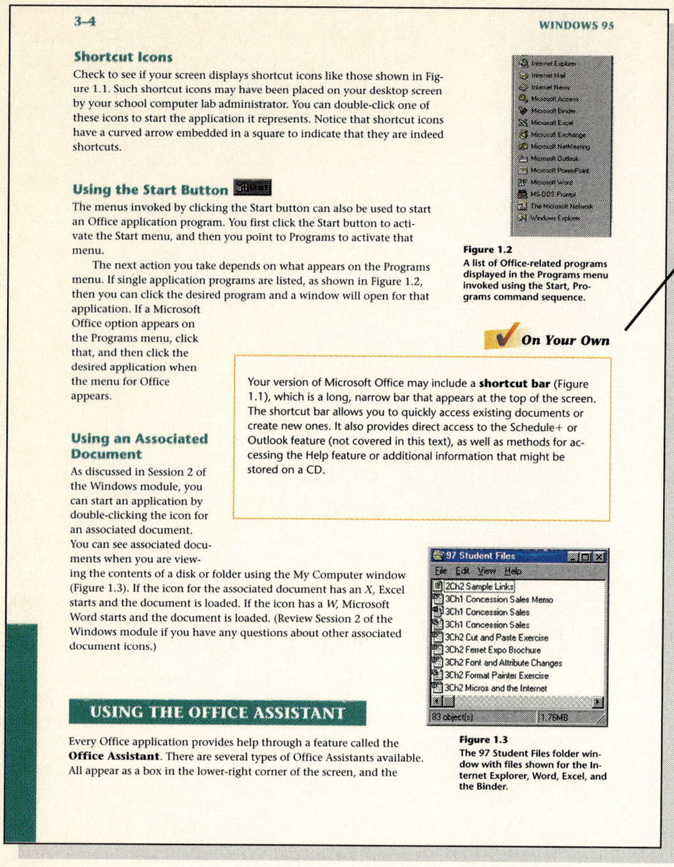

3–4 WINDOWS 95

Shortcut Icons

Check to see if your screen displays shortcut icons like those shown in Figure 1.1. Such shortcut icons may have been placed on your desktop screen by your school computer lab administrator. You can double-click one of these icons to start the application it represents. Notice that shortcut icons have a curved arrow embedded in a square to indicate that they are indeed shortcuts.

Using the Start Button

The menus invoked by clicking the Start button can also be used to start an Office application program. You first click the Start button to activate the Start menu, and then you point to Programs to activate that menu.

The next action you take depends on what appears on the Programs menu. If single application programs are listed, as shown in Figure 1.2, then you can click the desired program and a window will open for that application. If a Microsoft Office option appears on the Programs menu, click that, and then click the desired application when the menu for Office appears.

Figure 1.2
A list of Office-related programs displayed in the Programs menu invoked using the Start, Programs command sequence.

On Your Own

Your version of Microsoft Office may include a **shortcut bar** (Figure 1.1), which is a long, narrow bar that appears at the top of the screen. The shortcut bar allows you to quickly access existing documents or create new ones. It also provides direct access to the Schedule+ or Outlook feature (not covered in this text), as well as methods for accessing the Help feature or additional information that might be stored on a CD.

Using an Associated Document

As discussed in Session 2 of the Windows module, you can start an application by double-clicking the icon for an associated document. You can see associated documents when you are viewing the contents of a disk or folder using the My Computer window (Figure 1.3). If the icon for the associated document has an *X*, Excel starts and the document is loaded. If the icon has a *W*, Microsoft Word starts and the document is loaded. (Review Session 2 of the Windows module if you have any questions about other associated document icons.)

Figure 1.3
The 97 Student Files folder window with files shown for the Internet Explorer, Word, Excel, and the Binder.

USING THE OFFICE ASSISTANT

Every Office application provides help through a feature called the **Office Assistant**. There are several types of Office Assistants available. All appear as a box in the lower-right corner of the screen, and the

On Your Own boxes encourage students to explore the full range of features available in Office 97 applications.

Hands-On Exercises, based on the Running Case, give step-by-step instructions for learning each application. Numerous screen captures and button icons show students exactly what they need to know.

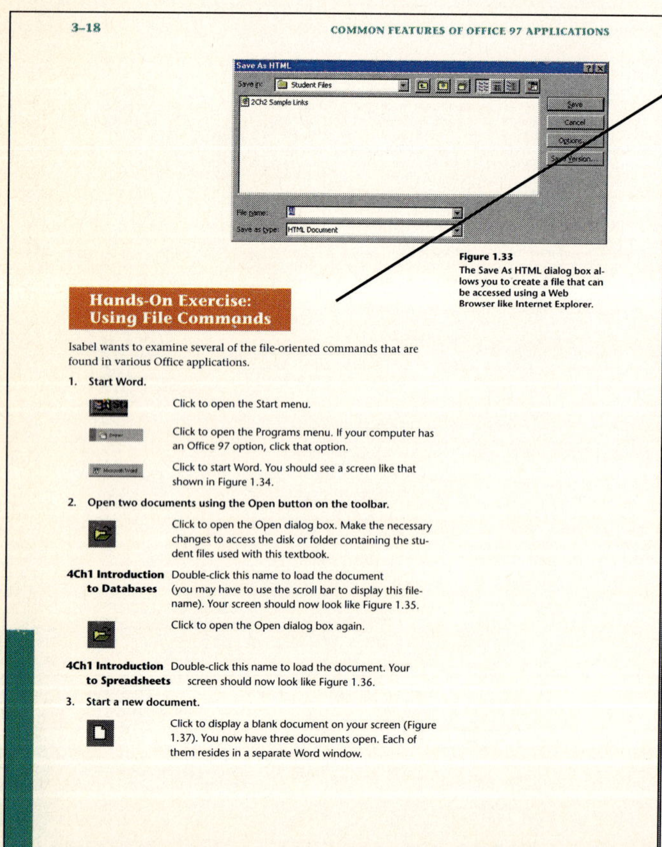

3–18 COMMON FEATURES OF OFFICE 97 APPLICATIONS

Figure 1.33
The Save As HTML dialog box allows you to create a file that can be accessed using a Web Browser like Internet Explorer.

Hands-On Exercise: Using File Commands

Isabel wants to examine several of the file-oriented commands that are found in various Office applications.

1. Start Word.

Click to open the Start menu.

Click to open the Programs menu. If your computer has an Office 97 option, click that option.

Click to start Word. You should see a screen like that shown in Figure 1.34.

2. Open two documents using the Open button on the toolbar.

Click to open the Open dialog box. Make the necessary changes to access the disk or folder containing the student files used with this textbook.

4Ch1 Introduction to Databases Double-click this name to load the document (you may have to use the scroll bar to display this file-name). Your screen should now look like Figure 1.35.

Click to open the Open dialog box again.

4Ch1 Introduction to Spreadsheets Double-click this name to load the document. Your screen should now look like Figure 1.36.

3. Start a new document.

Click to display a blank document on your screen (Figure 1.37). You now have three documents open. Each of them resides in a separate Word window.

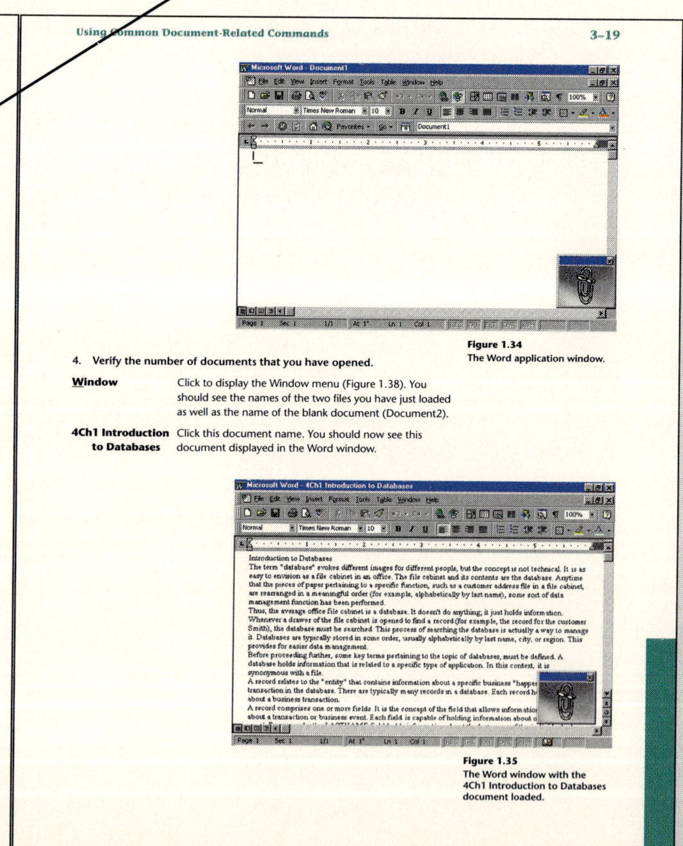

Using Common Document-Related Commands 3–19

Figure 1.34
The Word application window.

4. Verify the number of documents that you have opened.

Window Click to display the Window menu (Figure 1.38). You should see the names of the two files you have just loaded as well as the name of the blank document (Document2).

4Ch1 Introduction to Databases Click this document name. You should now see this document displayed in the Word window.

Figure 1.35
The Word window with the 4Ch1 Introduction to Databases document loaded.

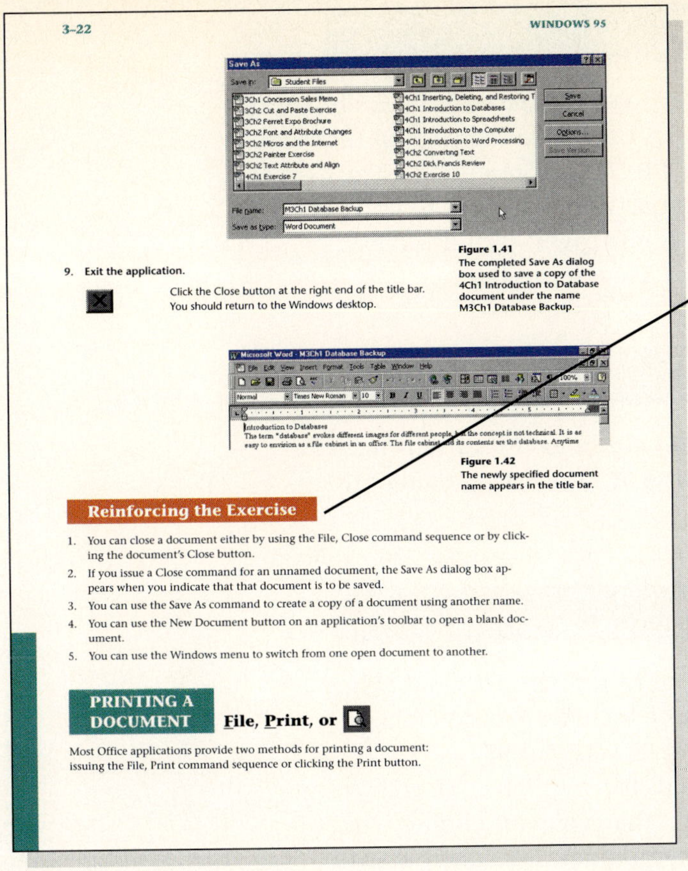

3–22 WINDOWS 95

Figure 1.41
The completed Save As dialog box used to save a copy of the 4Ch1 Introduction to Database document under the name M3Ch1 Database Backup.

9. Exit the application.

Click the Close button at the right end of the title bar. You should return to the Windows desktop.

Figure 1.42
The newly specified document name appears in the title bar.

Reinforcing the Exercise

1. You can close a document either by using the File, Close command sequence or by clicking the document's Close button.
2. If you issue a Close command for an unnamed document, the Save As dialog box appears when you indicate that that document is to be saved.
3. You can use the Save As command to create a copy of a document using another name.
4. You can use the New Document button on an application's toolbar to open a blank document.
5. You can use the Windows menu to switch from one open document to another.

PRINTING A DOCUMENT **File, Print, or**

Most Office applications provide two methods for printing a document: issuing the File, Print command sequence or clicking the Print button.

Reinforcing the Exercise sections help students recall and refer to the work they have completed.

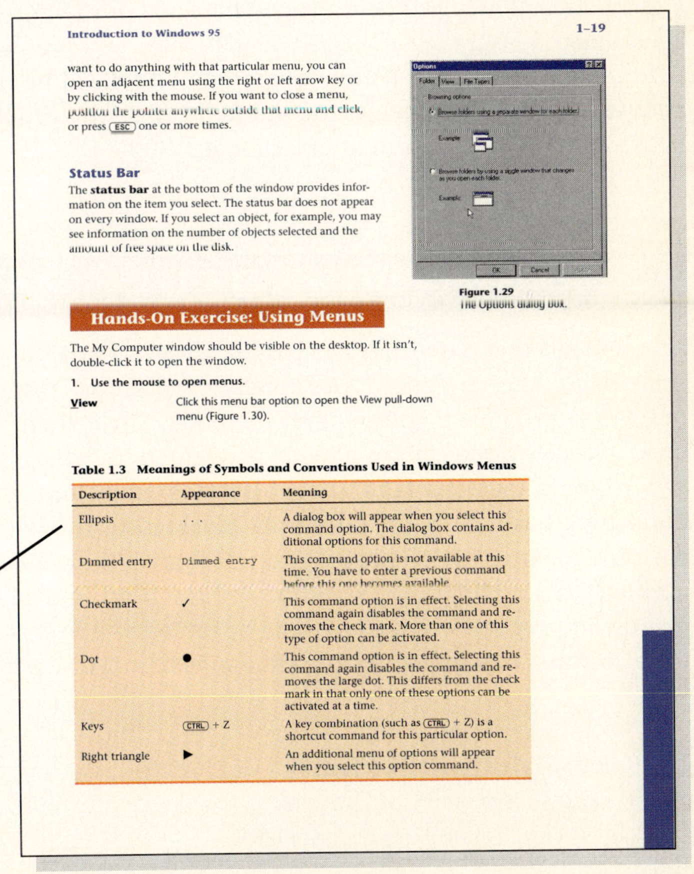

Introduction to Windows 95 1–19

want to do anything with that particular menu, you can open an adjacent menu using the right or left arrow key or by clicking with the mouse. If you want to close a menu, position the pointer anywhere outside that menu and click, or press ESC one or more times.

Status Bar

The **status bar** at the bottom of the window provides information on the item you select. The status bar does not appear on every window. If you select an object, for example, you may see information on the number of objects selected and the amount of free space on the disk.

Figure 1.29
The Options dialog box.

Hands-On Exercise: Using Menus

The My Computer window should be visible on the desktop. If it isn't, double-click it to open the window.

1. Use the mouse to open menus.

View — Click this menu bar option to open the View pull-down menu (Figure 1.30).

Table 1.3 Meanings of Symbols and Conventions Used in Windows Menus

Description	Appearance	Meaning
Ellipsis	. . .	A dialog box will appear when you select this command option. The dialog box contains additional options for this command.
Dimmed entry	Dimmed entry	This command option is not available at this time. You have to enter a previous command before this one becomes available.
Checkmark	✓	This command option is in effect. Selecting this command again disables the command and removes the check mark. More than one of this type of option can be activated.
Dot	●	This command option is in effect. Selecting this command again disables the command and removes the large dot. This differs from the check mark in that only one of these options can be activated at a time.
Keys	CTRL + Z	A key combination (such as CTRL + Z) is a shortcut command for this particular option.
Right triangle	▶	An additional menu of options will appear when you select this option command.

Tables of keyboard or **toolbar icons and symbols** provide students with a quick reference to the conventions and uses of Office 97 applications.

WEB SUPPORT

The Web site created for this text is **http://www.awl.com/office97/**. The site provides an interactive experience for students as they complete exercises in the text that send them to the site for information or files. Duffy teaches students how to view and save graphics, how to navigate on the Web, and how to download files; he even offers help on creating their own home pages. Web-based exercises appear at the end of each session in the Internet Exercises section.

ANCILLARIES

The **Instructor's Manual** offers teaching notes to help integrate current technology (such as the text Web site) into a modern course on Office 97, grading tips, and answer keys.

TECHSUITE PROGRAM

Office 97 applications texts are available separately or in a single *Microsoft Office 97 Professional* volume. The Office 97 Professional suite includes Windows 95, Internet Explorer 3.0, Word 97, Access 97, Excel 97, and PowerPoint 97.

Addison-Wesley realizes that you have specific needs for your lab course, so we offer the quick and affordable TechSuite program so that you can choose what you want. Your choice of lab manuals will be sent to your bookstore, combined in a TechSuite, allowing students to purchase all books in one convenient package at a discount.

Your Addison Wesley Longman representative will be happy to work with you and your bookstore manager to outline the ordering process and provide pricing, ISBNs, and delivery information. Or call 1-800-447-2226 or visit our Web site at http://www.awl.com/he/is/.

ACKNOWLEDGMENTS

I am amazed that ten years have passed since I started the first edition of *Four Software Tools*. At that time, I was totally unaware of the time-consuming efforts needed to produce a college-level textbook. Since then, however, I have developed a sincere appreciation of what is required to make a successful text. The success formula includes family, friends, colleagues, and many individuals in the publishing business. I remain deeply indebted to my wife, Wendy, who encouraged me to write the original version of *Four Software Tools*. Without her encouragement, the original text would never have been finished, and without her continued support, these projects would be impossible to accomplish.

I also want to express my sincere appreciation to the reviewers of this manuscript:

Jill Betts, Tyler Junior College
Bill Daley, University of Oregon
Kathryn A. Drexel, Drexel Associates

Peter Drexel, Plymouth State College
Seth Hock, Columbus State Community College
Marie McCooey, Bryant College
Vincent J. Motto, Asnuntuck Community-Technical College
Stephen C. Solosky, Nassau Community College
Melinda C. White, Santa Fe Community College

Individuals at the publishing company also play an important role. Addison Wesley Longman's editorial staff is superb. With warm feelings, I would like to acknowledge Maureen Allaire, Carol Crowell, and Ed Moura. Maureen initially signed this book and over the years has had much to do with many of my books. I am pleased to be working again with Carol Crowell, who brings a wealth of editorial experience in microcomputer texts. Ed Moura, Editor-in-Chief, brought a number of excellent ideas to this project. Kerry Connor, editorial assistant, made certain that everything was going on an even keel. Bess Deck, Juliet Silveri, Sue Purdy Pelosi and Barbara Conway made the publishing process smooth and professional.

An often overlooked ingredient in the success of textbooks is the publisher's marketing and sales staff. Michelle Hudson's experienced efforts in developing a marketing plan are greatly appreciated. I am convinced that the Addison Wesley Longman sales staff is one of the best in the business.

A dedication is not complete without including my son, Michael. Michael continues to make any writing project a challenge. His requests to go biking, swimming, or pursue a new interest are much appreciated. Michael especially likes to surf the Web to complete homework assignments and has become a ten-year-old master at ferreting out information from the Web.

CONTENTS

WINDOWS 95

Windows 95

SESSION 1

Introduction to Windows 95

After completing this session, you should be able to:

- Define a graphic user interface (GUI)
- Start the computer system and Windows
- Exit Windows and turn off the computer
- Identify and use various components of the Windows desktop
- Identify and use components of a window
- Identify and use the taskbar
- Use dialog boxes
- Start and use Windows application programs
- Use the Windows Help feature

THE WINDOWS 95 ENVIRONMENT

Windows 95 is the first true combination of operating system and graphic user interface for Intel-based computers. It makes it easier for you to use your computer and the software that resides on that computer. An **operating system** is a complex set of computer instructions that lies between you, the person using the computer, and the computer itself. It accepts a command from the user, evaluates that command, and then executes the command. It is the operating system that makes a computer usable for human beings.

A **graphic user interface (GUI)** is a software program that allows you to communicate with your computer by using a pointing device called a **mouse.** In most instances, a mouse allows you to perform a task more quickly than a text-based environment, in which you perform tasks by entering many keystrokes from the keyboard.

Prior to the introduction of Windows 95, you had to first start the computer, which then loaded the disk operating system. A **disk operating system (DOS)** is a set of programs that allows the user to interact with the computer. After the operating system started, the older Windows program began. In this type of environment, you had to know how to use both DOS and Windows.

Windows 95, introduced in August 1995, folds DOS into a new GUI. This means that you only need to know how to use the Windows graphic user interface. In addition, the easy-to-understand version of the Windows GUI allows a beginner to get started quickly using a computer and learning how to use and interact with application software.

TIMELY TIP

Many computers in a classroom environment are hooked to local area networks and require that each student log onto the system using a special user name or identification (ID) and password. If you are operating in such an environment, your instructor will provide you with a logon ID. You will determine your password. Do not tell anyone your password, because anyone who knows your password can log onto the system with your name.

In this type of environment, after Windows starts, a box appears requesting your user name and password. Enter your user name. Press TAB to move the cursor to the Password text box, and enter your password. The letters that you type do not appear in the box (they are replaced by asterisks), because you don't want any other people to see your password.

After you have finished entering this information, Windows finishes loading.

Starting Windows

To start Windows 95, you just start your computer. Once you turn on the computer, Windows 95 loads automatically. During this startup process, you may see a screen that looks like a Microsoft flag. When Windows has completely loaded you will see a screen called the desktop.

The Windows Desktop

Once Windows has finished loading, the desktop appears on your screen. The **desktop** (Figure 1.1) is a workspace (much like the top of a desk) on which you can perform a variety of tasks. Images appearing here might allow you to start a program and open a document stored on your system.

This desktop provides a work area for each session that you have with Windows. When you start an application, it will appear as a window on the desktop. The desktop shown in Figure 1.1 may differ from the one currently on your screen. You may see a different background color and different items displayed. You can customize Windows in just about any way you want.

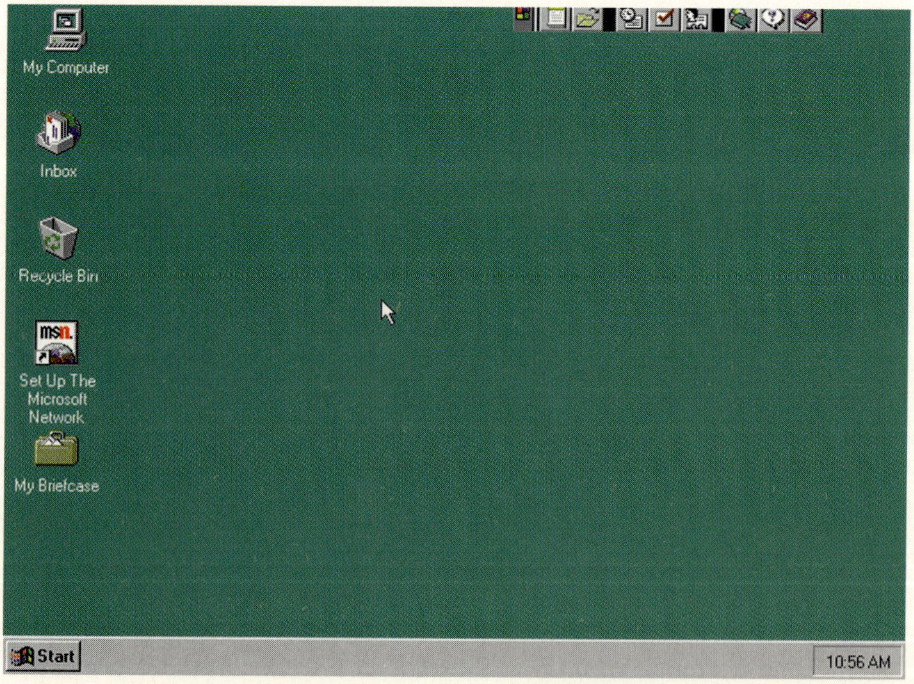

Figure 1.1
The Windows desktop.

Desktop Objects

Any image or item that appears on the desktop is called an **object.** As we progress through the various modules in this text, you will see many different types of objects, including documents, fields in a database, and buttons on a toolbar. A graphic representation of an object is called an **icon.** Common icons on the desktop include My Computer, Inbox, Recycle Bin, and Network Neighborhood.

An object always has properties. **Properties** control how an object behaves and operates in a Windows environment. You control the properties of an object via a properties sheet. (You will learn more about properties when you use the applications in later modules.) The background color of the Windows desktop is an example of a property. For now, remember that all Windows applications make use of the concepts of objects, and all objects have properties.

EXAMINING THE WINDOWS DESKTOP

In the Windows 95 environment, you make extensive use of the mouse as a pointing device and as a method of entering many different commands. While this environment does allow you to use the keyboard, it is very cumbersome compared to the mouse.

The mouse pointer is a large white arrow that appears on-screen. This image moves as you move the mouse on your workspace. You can use a mouse to take the actions listed in Table 1.1.

Table 1.1 Mouse Actions

Action	Description
Point	Move the mouse so that the pointer rests on a part of the screen (an icon or command, for instance).
Click	Quickly press and release the left mouse button. Click an object to select it. To deselect something, click any unused area of the desktop.
Right-click	Use the right button to invoke a context menu, as shown in Figure 1.2. This menu shows the most frequently used commands for that object. To get rid of the context menu, click any unused area of the desktop.
Double-click	Press and release the left mouse button twice rapidly in succession. You often use this operation to start an application represented by an icon.
Drag	Press and hold the left mouse button while moving the mouse. Use this operation to include multiple lines or cells in a selected block to be operated on by a subsequent command. It can also be used to move an object to another location.
Deselect	Click anywhere on a blank area of the screen.

Table 1.2 Pointer Shapes and Their Meanings

Shape	Meaning	Shape	Meaning
	Normal Select		Unavailable
	Help Select		Vertical Resize
	Working in Background		Horizontal Resize
	Busy		Diagonal Resize 1
	Precision Select		Diagonal Resize 2
	Text Select		Move
	Handwriting		Alternate Select

Unless you have set up (or configured) Windows differently, you will use the left mouse button to issue any instructions. Some people configure Windows to switch the buttons and, therefore, use the opposite button than the one indicated.

When you are using the mouse, the shape of the pointer provides valuable information. For instance, the shape of the pointer tells you when you are performing a normal selection, selecting text, resizing a window, or moving a window. Various possible shapes of the pointer are shown in Table 1.2.

TIMELY TIP

A computer mouse can have many different characteristics. It may, for example, have three mouse buttons. If that is the case, the middle button is programmable, or user-definable. This book makes use of only the left and right mouse buttons, regardless of whether you use a two- or three-button mouse.

You can also substitute a trackball for a mouse. A trackball is similar to a mouse except that it appears to be upside down, with the ball on the top. The advantage of a trackball is that you do not need an area of your workspace cleared to move the mouse around. A trackball can also have either two or three buttons.

Hands-On Exercise: Using the Mouse

1. **Practice moving the mouse.** Get a feel for how your hand movement affects the movement of the pointer. As you perform the following exercises, notice how the pointer moves on-screen.
   a. Move the mouse away from you.
   b. Move the mouse toward you.
   c. Move the mouse to the right.
   d. Move the mouse to the left.
   e. Move the mouse diagonally.

Practice moving the pointer on the screen until you feel comfortable using the mouse.

TIMELY TIP

> In this text, the term *click* means to click the left mouse button and has the same effect as pressing ENTER. The term *right-click* means to click the right mouse button and is done to activate a context menu containing properties and options related to the selected object. An example of such a menu can be seen in Figure 1.2.

Figure 1.2
A sample context menu generated by clicking the right mouse button.

2. Select an object.

Position the pointer on the My Computer icon.

Click — Click the left mouse button to select the My Computer object. The icon should now appear blue, indicating that it has been selected. Note the position of this icon.

Drag — Click and drag the My Computer icon to the lower-left corner of the desktop (Figure 1.3).

Drag — Drag the My Computer icon back to its original location at the top of the screen.

Figure 1.3
The My Computer icon in a new location on the desktop.

3. Deselect the My Computer icon.

Click	Click anywhere in the blank area of the desktop to deselect the icon.

4. Open a context menu.

Right-click	Place the pointer in an unused area of the desktop and click the right mouse button. A context menu appears (Figure 1.4).

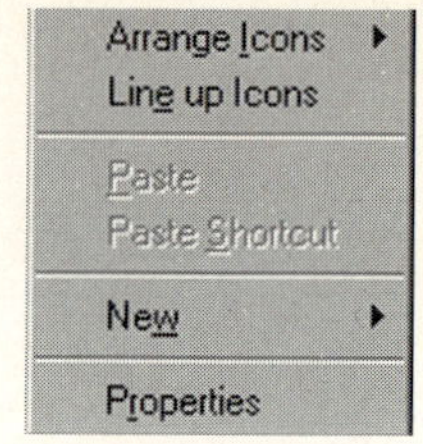

Figure 1.4
The context menu for the desktop.

5. Close the context menu.

Click	Place the pointer in an unused area of the desktop and click the left mouse button.

6. Open the context menu for the My Computer object.

Right-click	Place the pointer on the My Computer icon and click the right mouse button. The context menu appears as shown in Figure 1.5. Notice that the contents of the two context menus differ. The options that appear on the context menu depend on the object that you right-clicked.

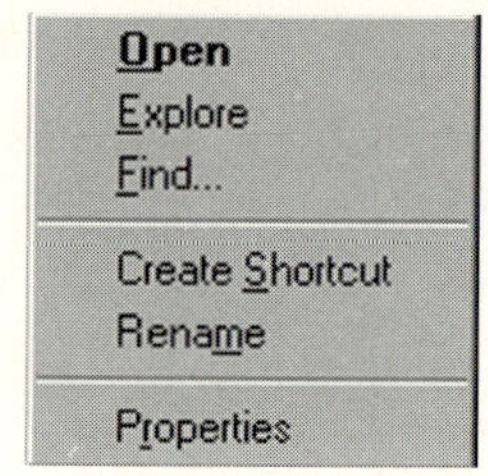

Figure 1.5
The context menu for the My Computer object.

7. Close the context menu.

Click	Place the pointer in an unused area of the desktop and click the left mouse button.

8. Open the My Computer window by double-clicking.

Double-click	Position the pointer on the My Computer icon and double-click the left mouse button. The window shown in Figure 1.6 appears. (The appearance and function of a window are discussed in more detail later in this session.)

9. Close the My Computer window.

Click the Close button in the upper-right corner of the My Computer window to close it.

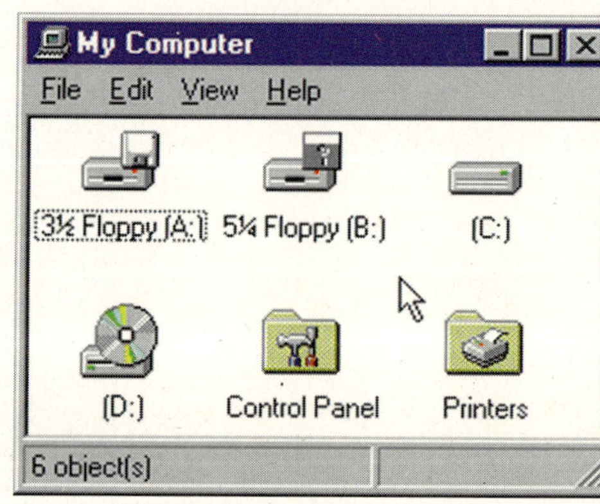

Figure 1.6
The My Computer window.

Reinforcing the Exercise

1. A context menu opens when you right-click an object.
2. To perform a drag operation, you click an object and continue holding down the left mouse button as you move the pointer.
3. Close a context menu by clicking any unused area of the desktop.
4. You open an object or application represented by an icon by double-clicking that icon.

Examining Some Desktop Objects

The following sections summarize some objects typically found on the Windows desktop.

My Computer

The My Computer icon opens a window that displays information about the resources of your computer, such as printers, the disk drive(s), fixed disk(s), and the CD-ROM drive, if any. By double-clicking on the icon that represents one of these storage devices, you can see what folders and files that device contains.

It also allows you to access system configuration data as well as any modem links to an Internet provider (if any have been installed on your computer).

Inbox

The Inbox icon allows you to access Microsoft's e-mail software, Exchange. You use this software to send and receive e-mail messages as well as faxes over a network or via an Internet provider. Your instructor will provide access information for Exchange, if it has been installed at your site.

Recycle Bin

The Recycle Bin provides a repository for deleted documents. With the Recycle Bin, you can easily restore documents you have inadvertently erased.

Taskbar

The **taskbar** (Figure 1.7) is the gray bar that always appears at the bottom of the desktop. As you will see later in this session, you can quickly shift from one application to another by clicking the application buttons displayed in the taskbar. The application buttons represent open windows or programs that have been started and are currently running in windows. The status area at the far right end of the taskbar displays miniature icons representing small programs that are always in memory (like the clock). The Start button appears at the far left end of the taskbar and is discussed separately below.

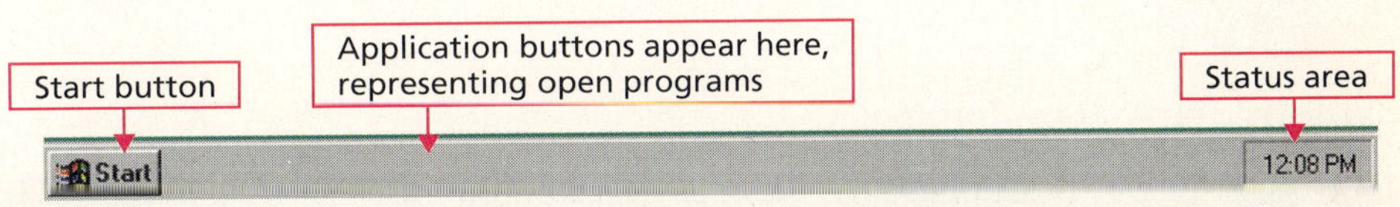

Figure 1.7
The taskbar for Windows 95.

Start Button

The Start button is located at the left end of the taskbar. It provides a click's access to programs, documents, settings, and other types of objects (Figure 1.8). It also provides the only safe way to exit Windows.

Opening Multiple Windows

Clicking or double-clicking an object on the desktop often causes a window to open. If one window already appears on-screen and you open another, the second window overlaps the first. This means that you may, at any time, have multiple windows visible on-screen. The window that appears on top is called the **active window.** Other windows beneath the active window are called **inactive windows.** When you click anywhere on an inactive window, it becomes the active window and has a colored rather than grey bar.

When you have multiple application windows open at one time, Windows is running each of these programs simultaneously. This Windows capability is called **multitasking.**

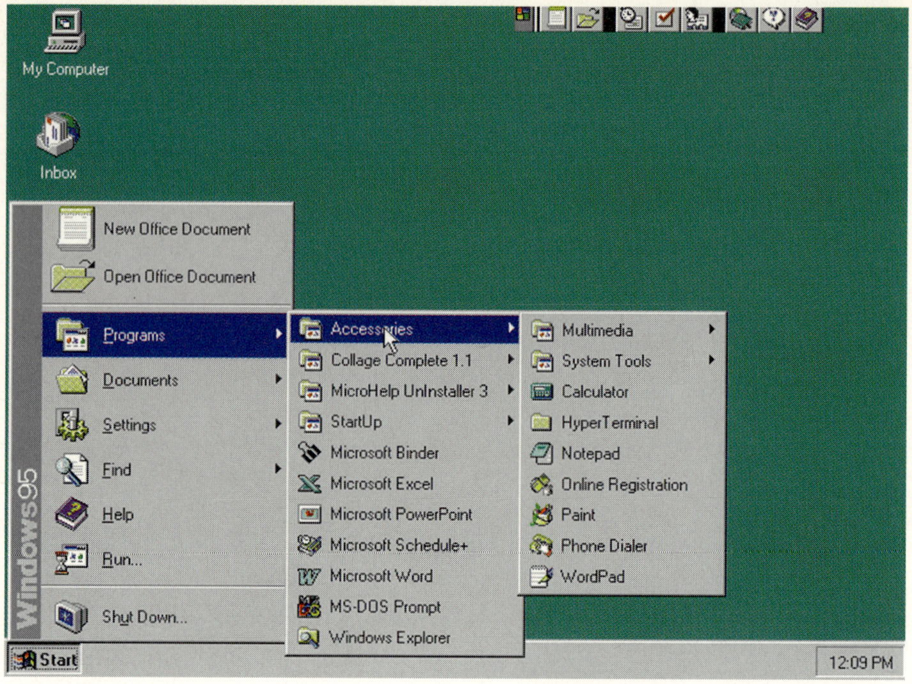

Figure 1.8
The Start button generates a series of menus, such as the Start, Programs, and Accessories menus.

Hands-On Exercise: Examining Windows Objects

1. Open the My Computer window.

Double-click

Double-click the My Computer icon. The My Computer window appears (Figure 1.9).

2. Open the window for drive C.

Double-click the drive C icon. (Your drive C icon may be labeled differently from that shown in Figure 1.9.) The window shown in Figure 1.10 appears, showing the contents of drive C. The folder icons represent other storage areas, while the other icons represent specific files of data. Notice that the two windows displayed overlap one another, and the drive C window is currently the active window.

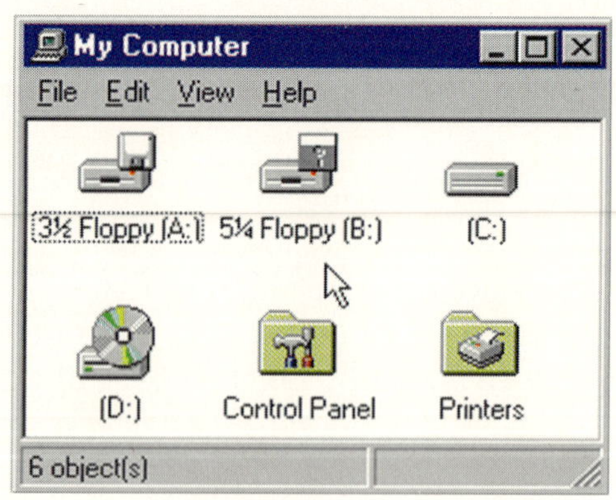

Figure 1.9
The My Computer window.

3. Make the My Computer window the active window.

Click

Click any part of the My Computer window. Your desktop should now appear as shown in Figure 1.11. Notice also that Windows has placed two buttons on the taskbar: one for the My Computer open window and the other for the drive C window. The icon for the active window appears highlighted.

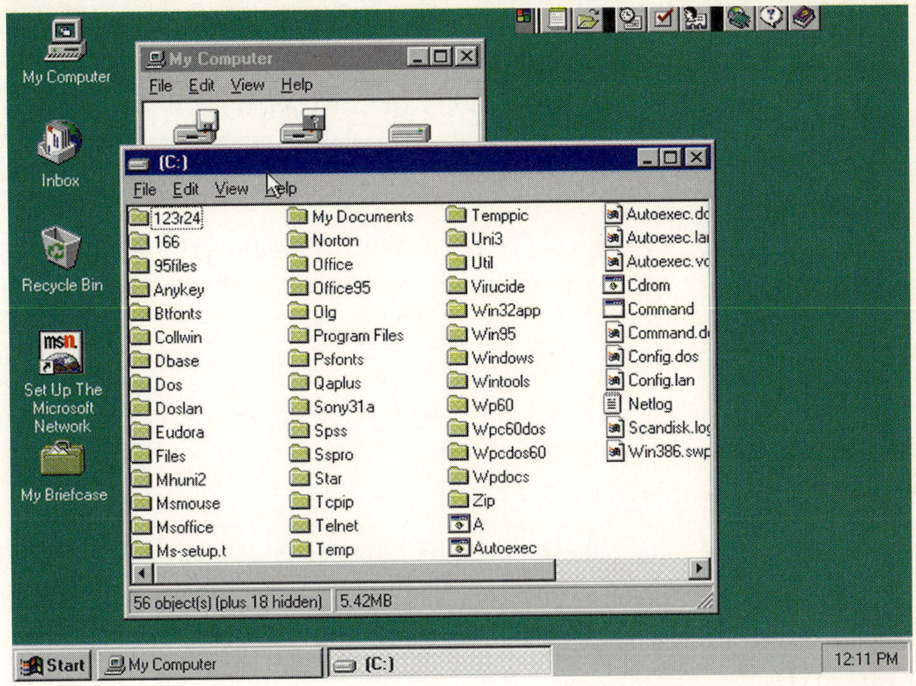

Figure 1.10
The window showing the contents of drive C. Note the buttons on the task bar.

4. **Close the two open windows.**

Click the Close button at the top of the My Computer window. The My Computer window should now disappear.

Click the Close button at the top of the drive C window. The drive C window should now disappear.

Figure 1.11
The Windows desktop with the active My Computer window on top of the drive C window.

5. **Examine any files that have been deleted recently.**

Position the pointer on the Recycle Bin icon and double-click the left mouse button. A window like that shown in Figure 1.12 should appear (you may see file names).

Figure 1.12
The Recycle Bin allows you to restore data that has been inadvertently deleted from your computer.

6. **Close the Recycle Bin window.**

Click the Close button at the top of the Recycle Bin window. The Recycle Bin window should now disappear.

7. **Open the Start menu.**

Click the Start button. The Start menu appears (Figure 1.13). Any menu option with an arrow to the right of it invokes another menu.

8. **Open the Programs menu.**

Point to the Programs option of the Start menu. A list of menu options starting with Accessories should appear to the right of the Start menu (Figure 1.14). Do not click on any of the menu options.

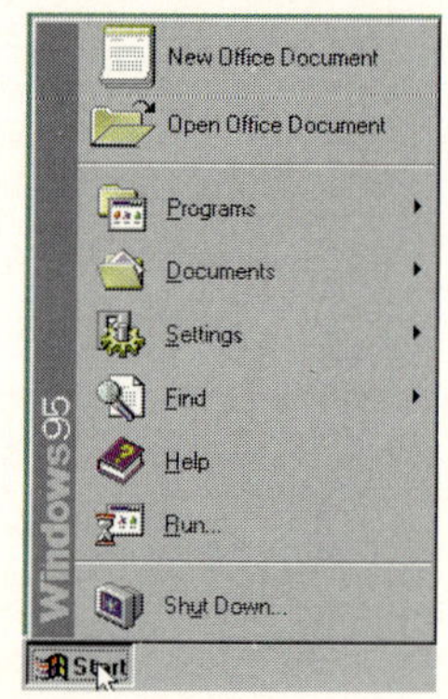

Figure 1.13
The Start menu opens when you click the Start button.

9. **Open the Accessories menu.**

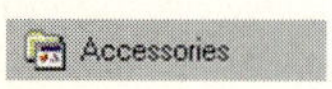

Point to the Accessories option with the mouse. The Accessories menu appears (Figure 1.15). Do not click on any of the options.

10. **Close the Start menu.**

Click — Click in an unused area of the desktop.

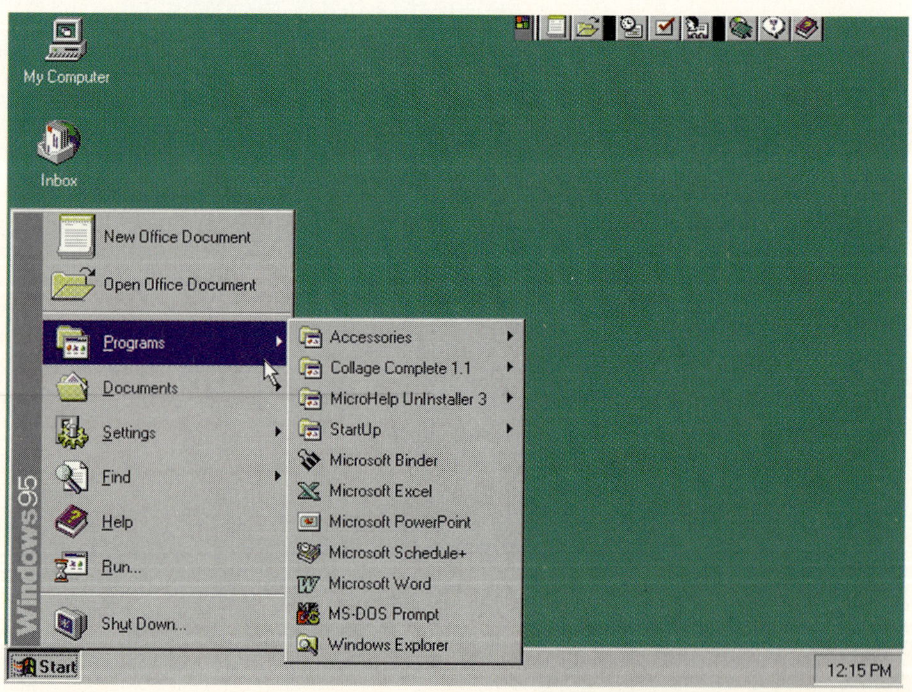

Figure 1.14
The Programs menu.

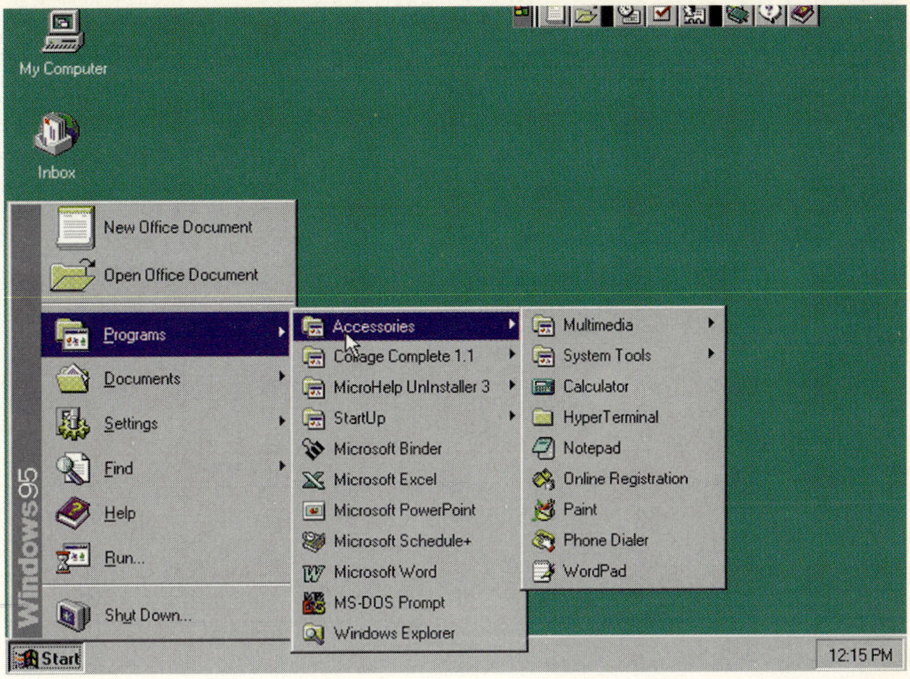

Figure 1.15
The Accessories menu.

Reinforcing the Exercise

1. The Start button is the starting point for all Windows programs, documents, and settings.
2. When you open a window, an application icon appears in the taskbar.
3. Documents you delete are stored in the Recycle Bin.
4. The My Computer window gives you information on the various resources of the computer, such as disk drives and printers.

EXITING WINDOWS

You must be careful to exit Windows properly before you turn off your computer. You should just turn off the power on your machine while Windows 95 is running. Windows uses many temporary files to perform its tasks and the tasks that you tell it to perform. These temporary files should be closed before you turn off your machine. You use the Shut Down Windows box (Figure 1.16) to close these files properly and exit Windows.

Exiting Windows requires the following steps:

Click the Start button to open the Start menu.

Choose Shut Down from the Start menu. The Shut Down Windows dialog box opens (Figure 1.16). The *Shut down the computer?* option is the default.

TIMELY TIP

If you inadvertently activate a program, click on the Close button in the upper-right corner of that application window.

Click the Yes button in the Shut Down Windows dialog box. You must wait until the message "It is now safe to turn off your computer" appears in big letters on your screen. Depending on how your computer is set up, you may have to wait up to four minutes. Once the message appears, you can turn off the computer.

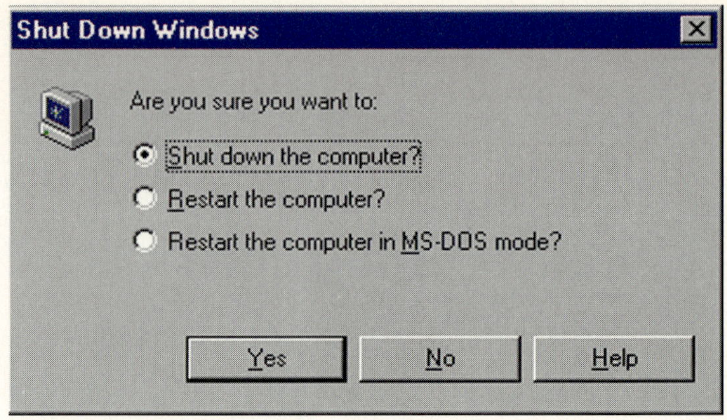

Figure 1.16
The Shut Down Windows dialog box provides various options for exiting Windows.

If you are using a computer hooked up to a local area network in a classroom lab, you will probably want to click the *Close all programs and log on as a different user* option. Choosing this option displays a dialog box that the next student will use to log onto Windows. Anything that a subsequent student does on the computer will be traced back to them instead of you.

Hands-On Exercise: Exiting Windows

1. Go through the steps for properly shutting down the computer.

Click to display the Start menu.

Click to display the Shut Down Windows dialog box. Notice that the *Shut down the computer?* option is automatically selected. If you were truly shutting down your computer, you would now click the Yes button.

2. Return to Windows.

Click to return to Windows.

TIMELY TIP

When several buttons appear on the taskbar, you can click a button to move from one window or application to another.

Reinforcing the Exercise

1. You should properly shut down a computer running Windows or risk damaging temporary files Windows uses to operate.
2. Start the shut down procedure by clicking the Start button.
3. If you are on a network and want to log on, you select *Close all programs and log on as a different user* from the Shut Down Windows box.

PARTS OF A WINDOW

The following sections summarize the parts of a typical window, the My Computer window shown in Figure 1.17.

Window Borders

The window **border** shows the limits of the window. You can **resize a window** by using a drag operation on the window border: First you position the pointer on a border line. The pointer turns into a two-headed arrow. You can then drag that border to resize the window.

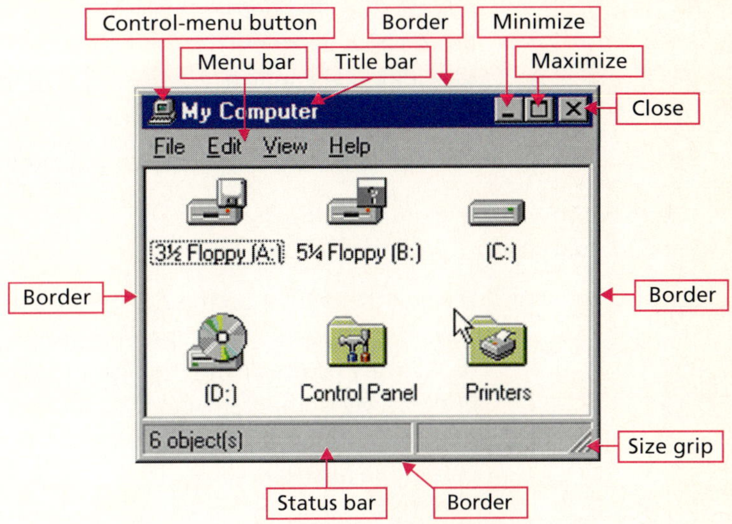

Figure 1.17
The parts of the My Computer window.

Size Grip 

The **size grip** icon, located in the lower-right corner, is a reference point that you can also use to resize a window easily. When you position the pointer on a size grip, the pointer changes to a double-headed arrow. You can then resize the window with a drag operation.

Hands-On Exercise: Changing a Window's Size

1. Open the My Computer window.

Double-click — Position the pointer on the My Computer icon and double-click the mouse. Your screen should now look similar to Figure 1.18.

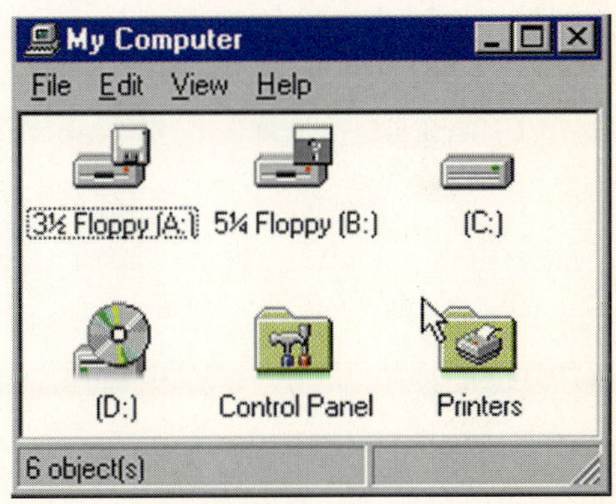

Figure 1.18
The My Computer window open and ready to be resized.

2. Make the My Computer window wider.

Drag ↔ — Position the pointer on the right window border. The pointer should turn into the Horizontal Resize pointer. Drag the border to the right about 1.5 inches. The My Computer window should now look like that shown in Figure 1.19.

3. Make the window taller.

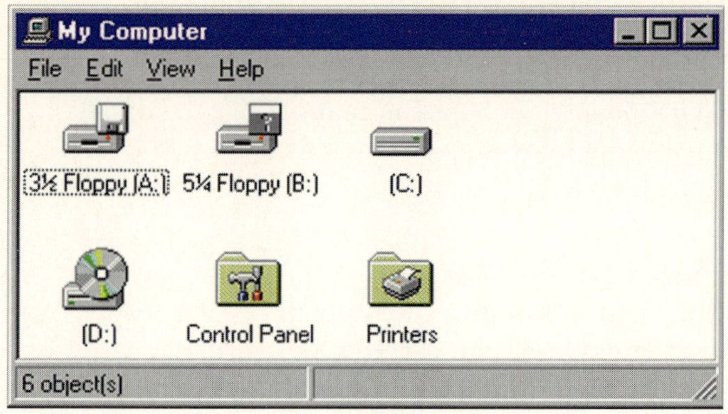

Figure 1.19
The widened My Computer window.

Drag

Position the pointer on the bottom border of the window. The pointer should turn into the Vertical Resize pointer. Drag the border down about 2 inches. The My Computer window should now look like that shown in Figure 1.20.

4. Return the My Computer window back to its original size.

Drag

Position the pointer on the size grip in the lower-right corner of the window. The pointer turns into the Diagonal Resize 1 pointer. Drag the size grip up and to the left until the My Computer window is returned to its original size. Leave the My Computer window open for the next part of the discussion.

Reinforcing the Exercise

1. Using the mouse, you can drag a window border to resize the window.
2. During a resizing operation, the pointer changes to a double-headed arrow.
3. The icon in the lower-right corner of a window is called the size grip.

Title Bar

The top of the window contains a colored bar (typically blue) called the **title bar.** The title bar contains the name of the open application, and three buttons you can use to control the window: the control-menu button, the Minimize button, the Maximize or Restore button, and the Close button.

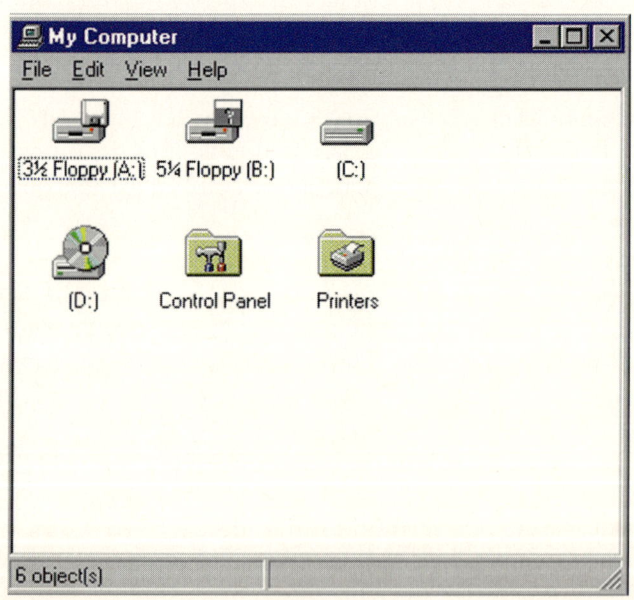

Figure 1.20
The taller My Computer window.

The **control-menu button** at the left end of the title bar is a throwback to older versions of Windows and is now rarely used. When you click this button, a menu like that shown in Figure 1.21 appears. When you double-click the control-menu button, the window closes (the same as clicking the Close button). Using the Close button (discussed below) instead of the control-menu button is the preferred way to close a window.

When you click an application window's **Minimize button,** the window disappears and only a button representing the application window appears on the taskbar (at the bottom of the desktop). Clicking the **Maximize button** enlarges the window to take up the entire screen. On a window that has been maximized, the Maximize button is replaced by a Restore button. When you click the **Restore button,** the window returns to its previous size. You click the **Close button** to close the application window.

You can also use the title bar to move a window. This is accomplished by positioning the pointer anywhere in the title bar and then dragging the window to the desired location.

TIMELY TIP

> What if you have used the Minimize button to reduce an application window to a button on the taskbar and you want to get rid of that button? You must first open the application by clicking the appropriate taskbar button. When the application window appears, you can click the Close button of that application window to close it, and the button for that application disappears from the taskbar.

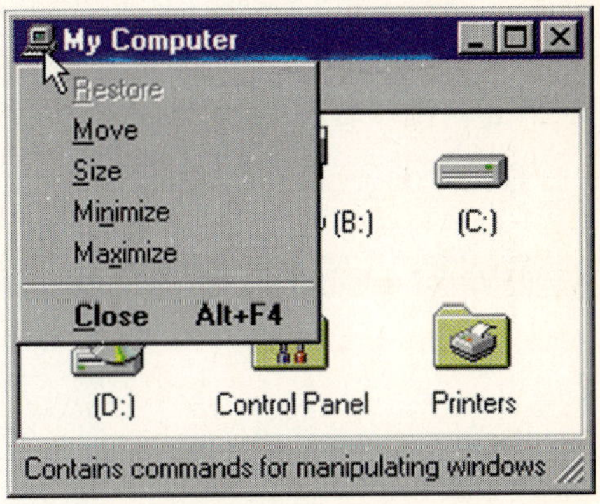

Figure 1.21
The control menu appears when you click the control-menu button.

Scroll Bar

A window may also have a vertical **scroll bar** on the right border (Figure 1.22). When you click the up or down arrow button, the screen moves up or down one line at a time. The position of the **scroll box** indicates the location of the cursor in the displayed text. You can drag the scroll box up or down to move the cursor quickly from one part of the screen to another. Clicking above or below the scroll box moves the information up or down one screen at a time.

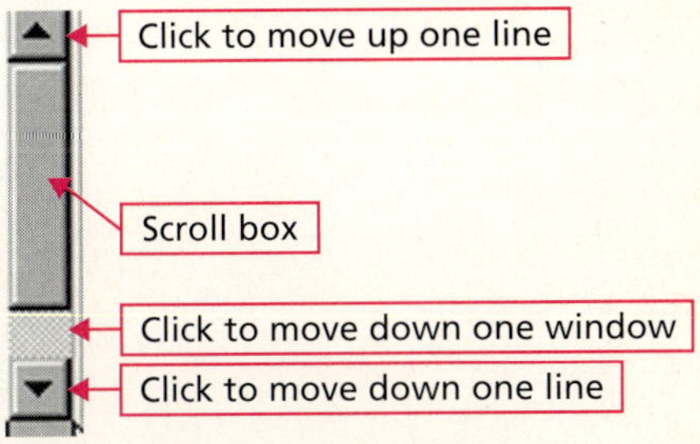

Figure 1.22
The parts of a scroll bar.

Hands-On Exercise: Using Title Bar Features

The My Computer window should still appear on the Windows desktop.

1. **Maximize the window.**

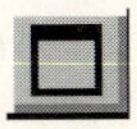

Click to make the My Computer window take up the entire desktop (Figure 1.23).

2. **Restore the window to its original size.**

Click to return the My Computer window to its original size (Figure 1.24).

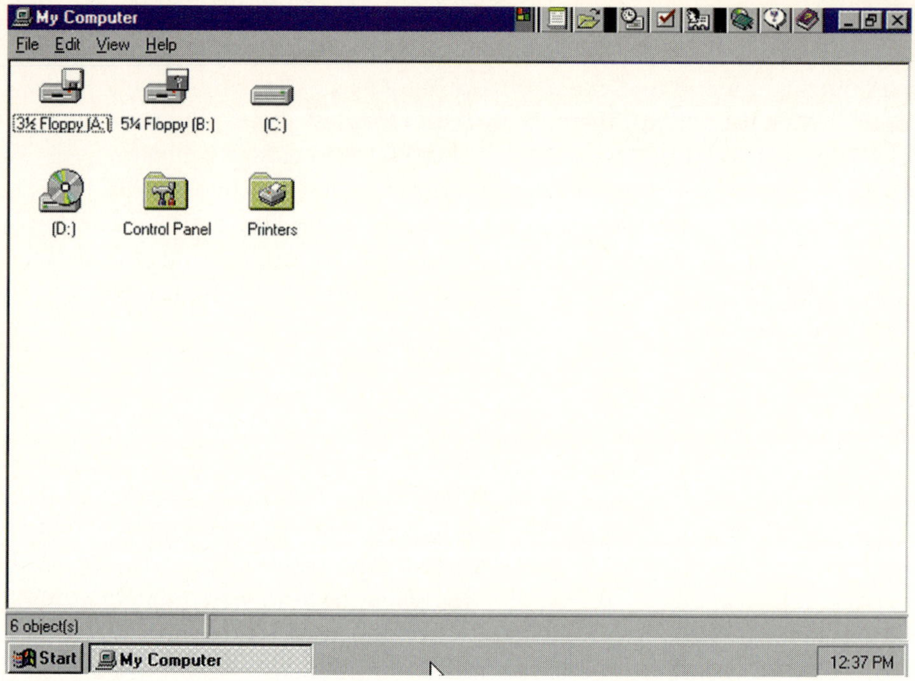

Figure 1.23
The maximized My Computer window.

3. **Minimize the My Computer window to a button on the taskbar.**

Click so that the only evidence of the My Computer window is a button on the taskbar (Figure 1.25).

4. **Open the My Computer window.**

Click to reopen the window.

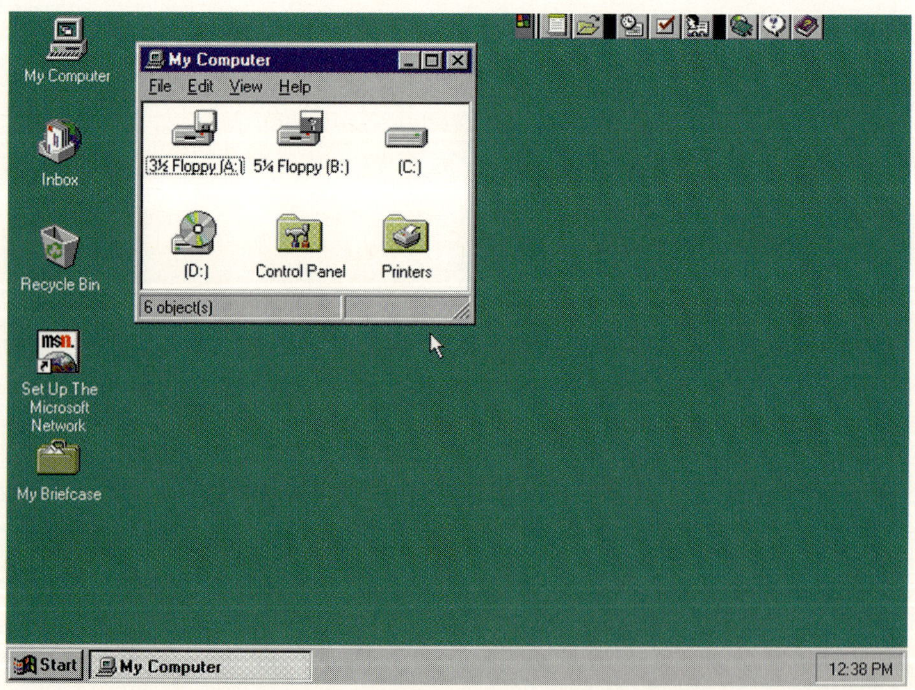

Figure 1.24
The restored My Computer window on the desktop.

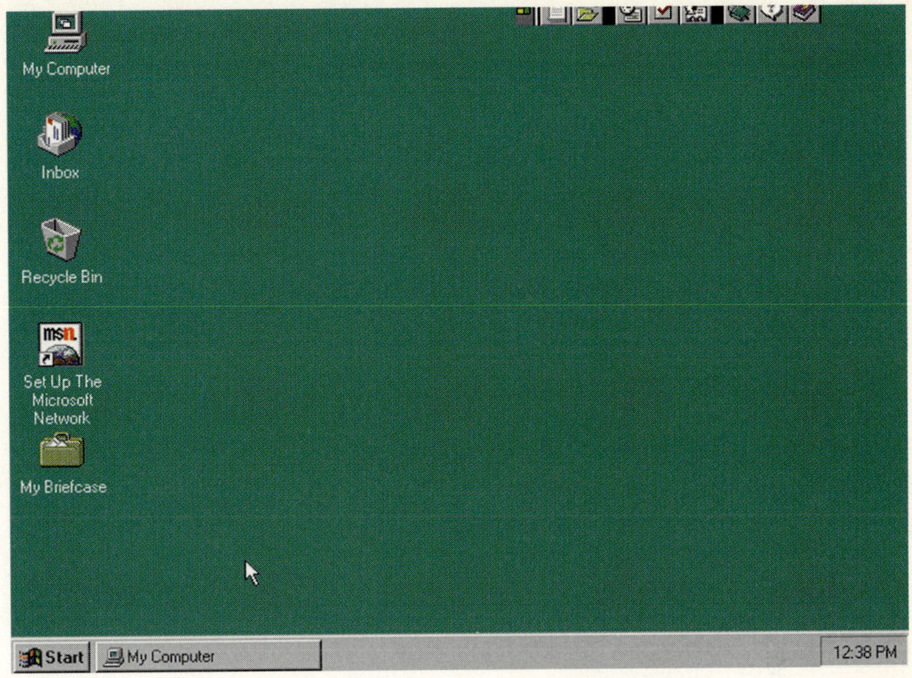

Figure 1.25
The My Computer window minimized to a taskbar button.

5. **Move the window.**

Position the pointer anywhere in the title bar of the My Computer window, and drag down and to the lower-right corner. The window moves with the pointer (Figure 1.26).

6. **Drag the window back to its prior location.**

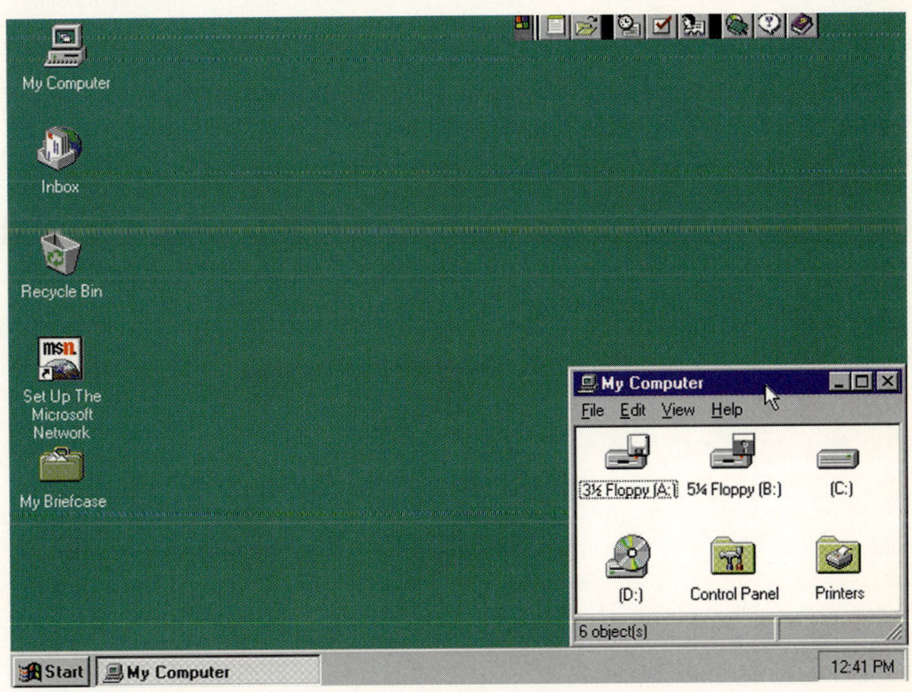

Figure 1.26
The My Computer window moved to the lower-right corner of the desktop.

Reinforcing the Exercise

1. Once a window is maximized, the Restore button replaces the Maximize button in the title bar.
2. To move a window on the desktop, you click anywhere in the title bar and drag the window.
3. When you click the Minimize button, the window is reduced to a button on the taskbar.
4. The recommended (and easiest) way to close a window is to click the Close button at the right end of the title bar.

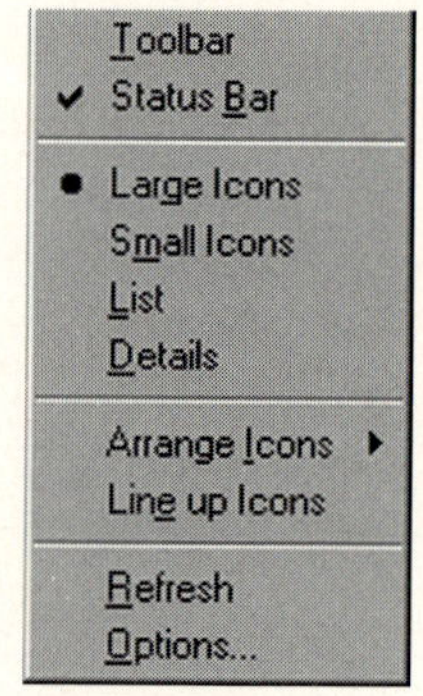

Figure 1.27
The View pull-down menu.

Menu Bar

The **menu bar** gives you access to the commands you need to work with in the window. Windows is consistent in how menus are arranged and in what types of commands, or options, are used in the menus from application to application. This consistency of menu display and use makes different Windows applications easier to learn.

You can open a menu from the menu bar by clicking the menu name. For example, when you click View in the menu bar, the View menu opens with a set of options for you to choose from (Figure 1.27). The menus you open from the menu bar are often called **pull-down menus.** You issue a command through a pull-down menu by clicking the appropriate option, by typing the letter that is underlined in the option name, or by using the arrow keys to highlight the option and then pressing Enter. When you choose an option that has a right arrow by its name, like Arrange Icons in the View menu, a new menu opens (Figure 1.28). When you choose a menu option that has an ellipsis (. . .) by its name, a dialog box appears (Figure 1.29). Table 1.3 lists the meanings of the symbols and conventions used in Windows menus.

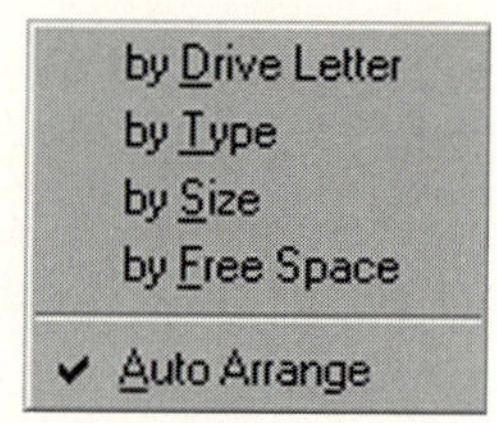

Figure 1.28
The new menu opened by choosing Arrange Icons from the View menu.

Alternatively, you can select menu options by typing **shortcut commands.** For example, the shortcut command that opens the View menu is ALT + V. Although you can issue shortcut commands from the keyboard, most computer novices find them cumbersome and difficult to memorize. Since Windows and applications that run in Windows are designed to be used with the mouse, you will primarily use the mouse in this text.

If you open a menu and then decide that you don't

TIMELY TIP

In this text, a series of menu selections is called a **command sequence.** For example, you invoke the View, Arrange Icons command sequence by first choosing View from the menu bar and then choosing Arrange Icons from the View menu.

want to do anything with that particular menu, you can open an adjacent menu using the right or left arrow key or by clicking with the mouse. If you want to close a menu, position the pointer anywhere outside that menu and click, or press (ESC) one or more times.

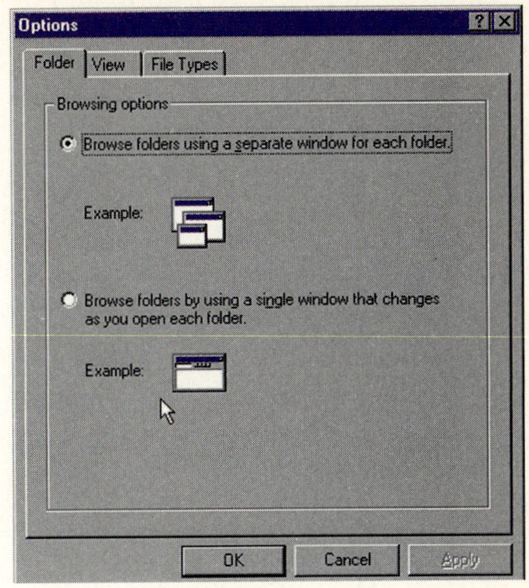

Figure 1.29
The Options dialog box.

Status Bar

The **status bar** at the bottom of the window provides information on the item you select. The status bar does not appear on every window. If you select an object, for example, you may see information on the number of objects selected and the amount of free space on the disk.

Hands-On Exercise: Using Menus

The My Computer window should be visible on the desktop. If it isn't, double-click it to open the window.

1. **Use the mouse to open menus.**

View Click this menu bar option to open the View pull-down menu (Figure 1.30).

Table 1.3 Meanings of Symbols and Conventions Used in Windows Menus

Description	Appearance	Meaning
Ellipsis	. . .	A dialog box will appear when you select this command option. The dialog box contains additional options for this command.
Dimmed entry	Dimmed entry	This command option is not available at this time. You have to enter a previous command before this one becomes available.
Checkmark	✓	This command option is in effect. Selecting this command again disables the command and removes the check mark. More than one of this type of option can be activated.
Dot	●	This command option is in effect. Selecting this command again disables the command and removes the large dot. This differs from the check mark in that only one of these options can be activated at a time.
Keys	(CTRL) + Z	A key combination (such as (CTRL) + Z) is a shortcut command for this particular option.
Right triangle	▶	An additional menu of options will appear when you select this option command.

TIMELY TIP

Throughout this text, the following system is used to show how keystrokes (if covered) are combined. When two or three keystrokes are separated by addition signs (such as CTRL + DEL), you must hold down the first key while you press the additional key or keys. When two keystrokes are separated by a comma (such as F2, DEL), simply press and release each key in the order given.

2. **Open the Arrange Icons menu.** The arrow to the right of the Arrange Icons option indicates a menu will appear.

Arrange Icons Click to display the Arrange Icons menu (Figure 1.31).

Click Click any unused area of the desktop to exit the menu.

3. **Open the Edit menu.**

Edit Point to this menu bar option. The Edit pull-down menu appears (Figure 1.32)

Click Click any unused area of the My Computer window to exit the menu.

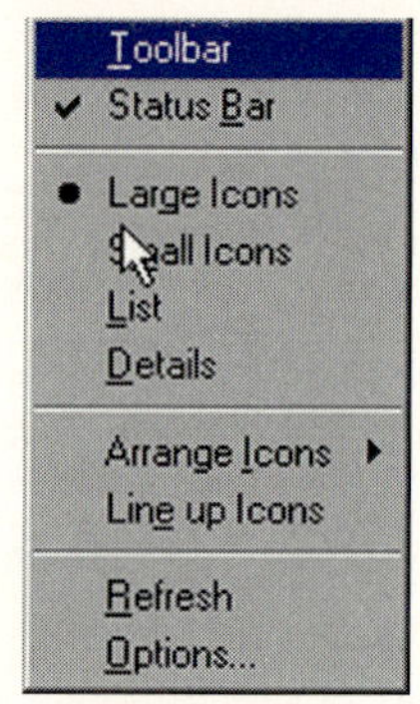

Figure 1.30
The options of the View menu.

4. **Open a menu using a context command.**

ALT + F Press this key combination to open the File pull-down menu (Figure 1.33).

5. **Open the View pull-down menu.**

→ (twice) Press the right arrow twice to open the View menu.

6. **Manually exit the menu.**

ESC Pressing ESC once closes the View menu. On the menu bar, the View option is still selected (Figure 1.34).

ESC Pressing ESC again returns control back to the desktop.

7. **Open a dialog box.**

View Click this menu bar option to open the View menu.

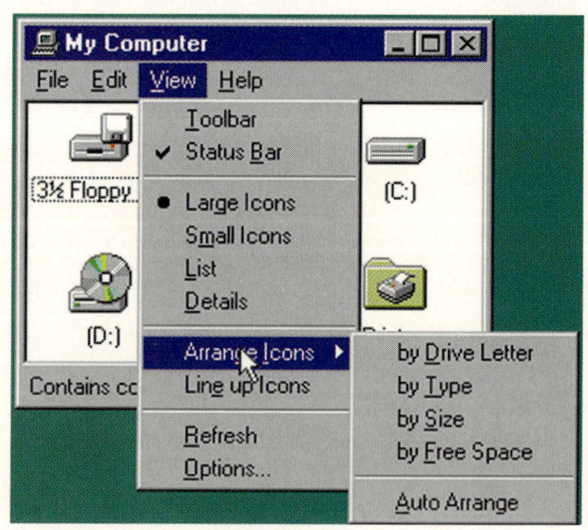

Figure 1.31
The options of the Arrange Icons menu.

Options. . . Click this View menu option to open the Options dialog box (Figure 1.35). The Folder tab should be on top. If it isn't, click it to activate it.

View Click to activate the View tab (Figure 1.36). Notice how the dialog box has changed to reflect the appearance of the active tab page.

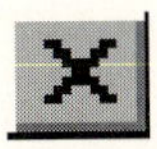
Click the Close button of the Options dialog box.

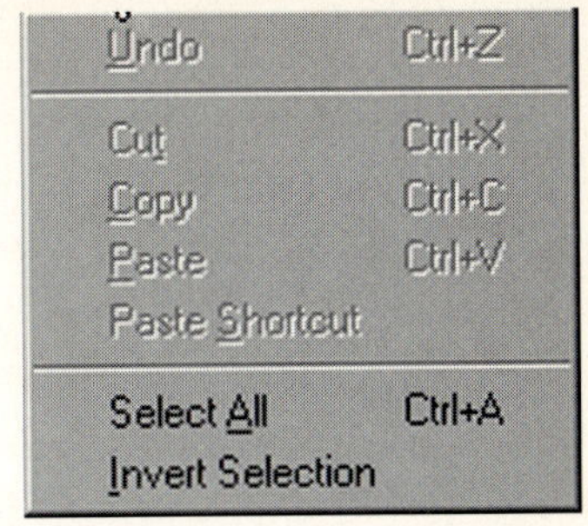

Figure 1.32
The Edit menu.

Reinforcing the Exercise

1. You can open a menu from the menu bar by clicking its name or by pressing ALT + the letter in its name that is underlined.
2. You close a menu by clicking anywhere on the desktop outside of the menu or by pressing ESC.
3. An ellipsis after an option name indicates that a dialog box will open when you select that option.
4. A right arrow after an option name indicates that another menu will open when you select that option.

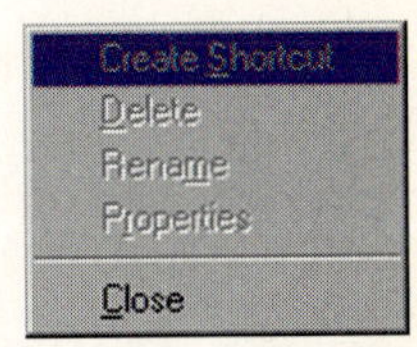

Figure 1.33
The File menu opened by issuing the ALT + F shortcut command.

Using Windows Dialog Boxes

As mentioned in the discussion of menus, a **dialog box** automatically appears on-screen after you select a menu option that has an ellipsis (...). For example, selecting the Options option from the View menu opens the dialog box shown in Figure 1.35. A dialog box is a window that prompts you for information it needs to carry out a command. A dialog box may, like the Options dialog box, have tabs that when clicked display a different part of the dialog box. In Figure 1.35, the Folder tab is active, and in Figure 1.36, the View tab is active.

A dialog box also contains controls. **Controls** allow you to interact with a dialog box or window. Common types of controls include text boxes, check boxes, list boxes, option buttons, command buttons, spin boxes, and various combinations of these elements. Figure 1.37 shows the Print dialog box with each of these controls labeled.

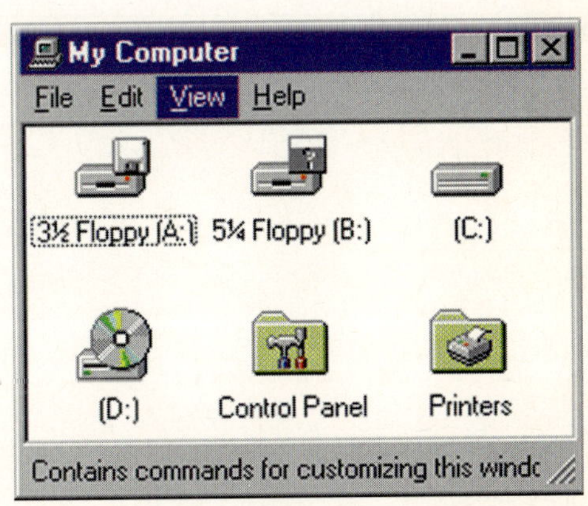

Figure 1.34
After you press ESC once, View is still highlighted on the menu bar.

Option Buttons

Option buttons turn options on or off. Only one option button can be on at once. A dot (●) next to an option shows which option button is selected.

List Boxes

A list box displays a list of options from which you can choose. To see the list, you may have to click the down arrow at the right end of the box. To select an option, you click it. If there are more items than will fit in the box, a scroll bar will appear on the right side of the list box to allow you to move through the list.

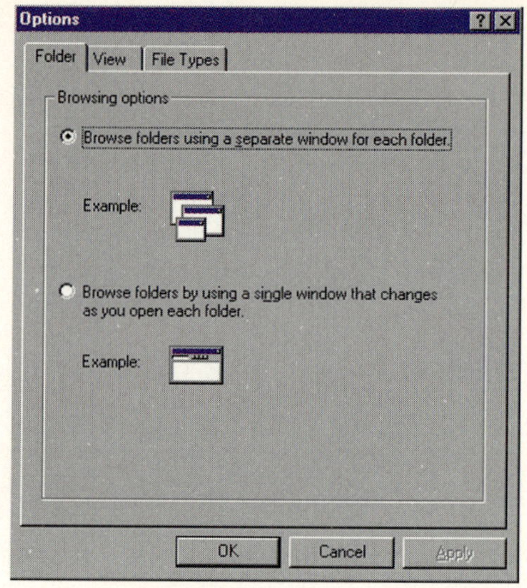

Figure 1.35
The Options dialog box with the Folder tab active.

Check Boxes

A check box turns an option on and off. A check in a check box means the option is on. Several check boxes can be active at one time. To check or uncheck an item, you click it.

Command Buttons

You issue commands by clicking command buttons in an open dialog box. Two common command buttons are OK and Cancel. OK confirms choices and closes the dialog box. Cancel ignores any choices that you made and closes the dialog box. A command button with an ellipsis (. . .) after its name takes you to another dialog box.

Text Boxes

A text box allows you to enter and edit information that is needed to perform a task, such as entering the name of a file. A text box may include the insertion point when the dialog box opens, or you can place the insertion point there by clicking inside the text box.

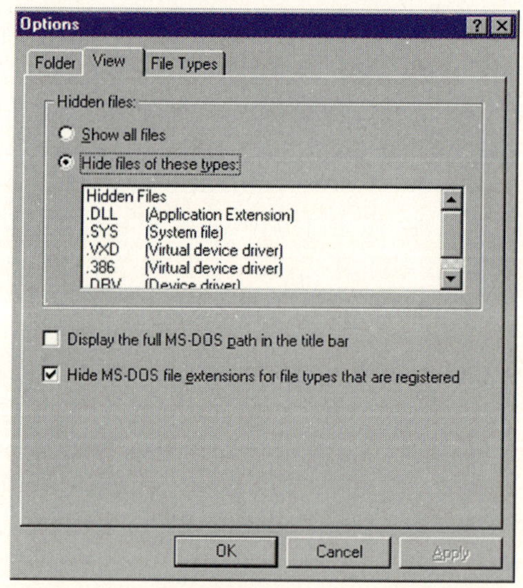

Figure 1.36
The Options dialog box with the View tab active.

Spin Boxes

A spin box is a control with a number and small up and down arrow icons to the right of the box. You click these arrows to increase or decrease the value contained in the spin box.

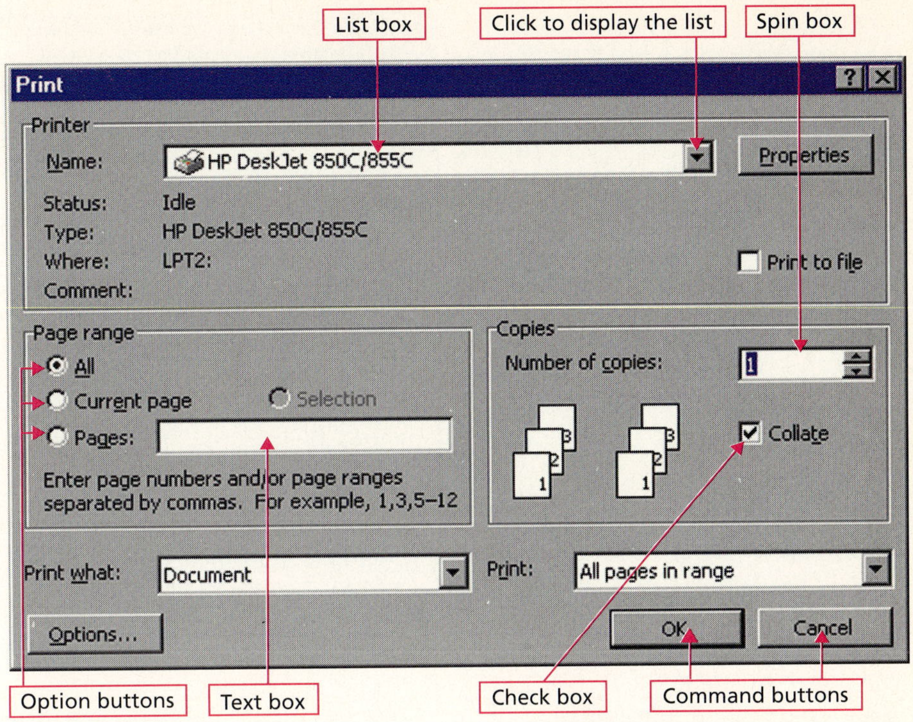

Figure 1.37
Word's Print dialog box contains a number of controls.

Hands-On Exercise: Using Dialog Boxes

1. **Start Word.**

Click the Start button. The Start menu appears.

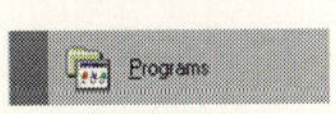

Point to this option to open the Programs menu.

Click to start Microsoft Word (Figure 1.38).

2. **Open the Print dialog box.**

File Click to open the File menu.

Print. . . Click to open the Print dialog box (Figure 1.39).

3. **Use the Copies spin box to determine the number of copies.**

Use the up arrow of the spin box to increase the number of copies to 6 (Figure 1.40).

Use the down arrow of the spin box to reset the number of copies back to 1.

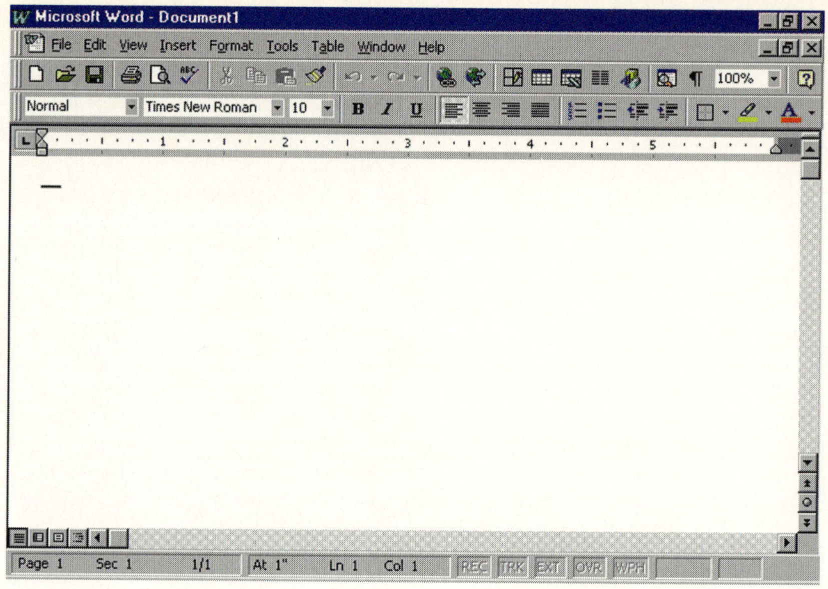

Figure 1.38
The Microsoft Word window.

4. **Use the option buttons.**

O Pages — Click to change the selection. Notice that All is no longer selected. Remember, when you are using option buttons, only one button can be active at any one time.

O All — Click to change the selection. Again, only one remains selected.

5. **Use a text box.**

O Pages — Click to change the selection.

Type: **4** — The number 4 should now appear in the Pages text box (Figure 1.41).

6. **Select from a selection box.**

Print what: — Point to the Print what list box. The current selection is Document.

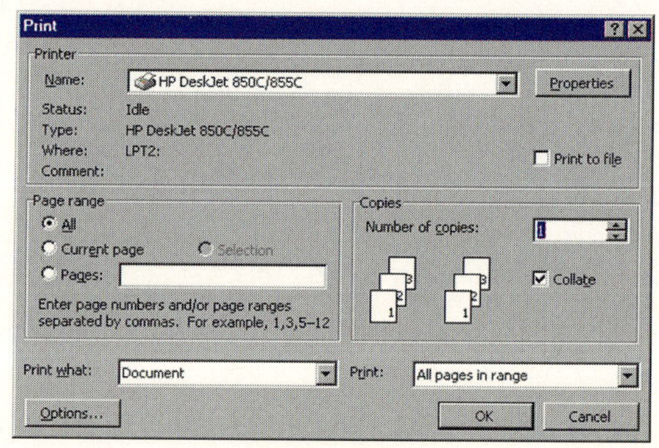

Figure 1.39
Word's Print dialog box.

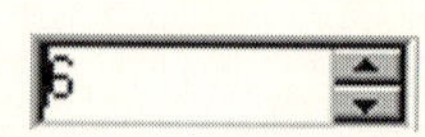

Figure 1.40
The spin box with the contents of 6.

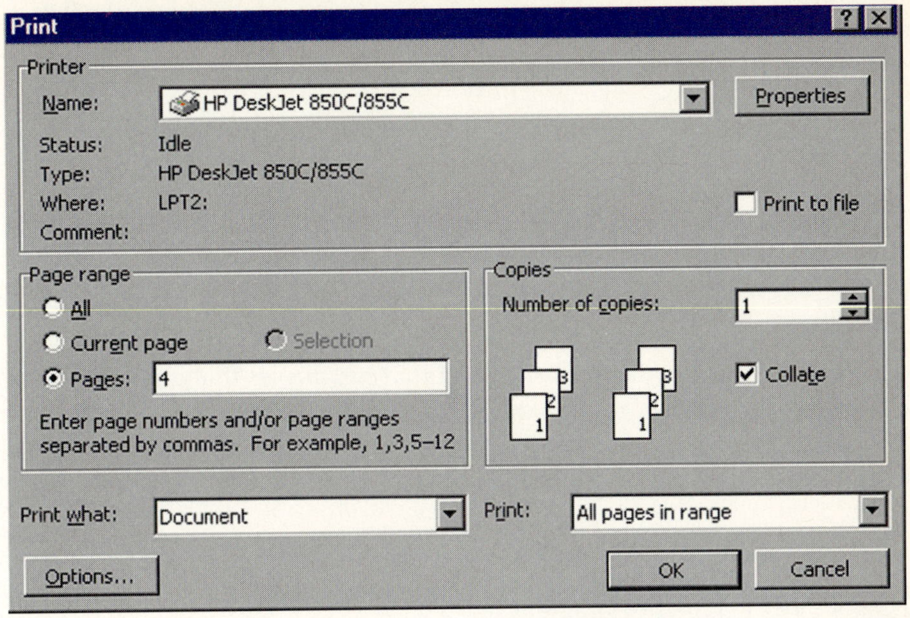

Figure 1.41
The Pages text box now contains a value of 4.

Click to display a list of options (Figure 1.42).

Styles Select "Styles" from the dropdown list box.

7. **Use a command button to exit the dialog box.**

Click the cancel button to return to the application window.

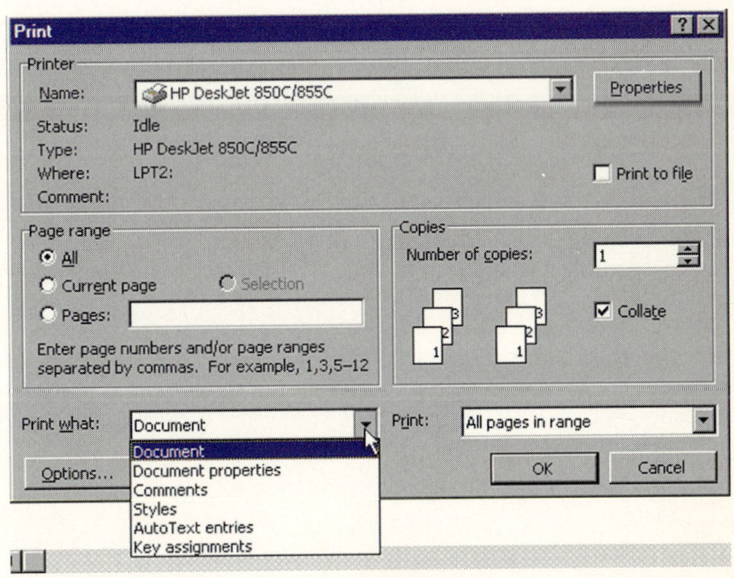

Figure 1.42
The Print what list box offers several alternatives of what to print.

8. Return to the desktop.

Click the Close button on the Microsoft Word title bar.

Reinforcing the Exercise

1. You use a dialog box to provide Windows with the information it needs to complete a command.
2. The spin box is a dialog box control that has arrows that allow you to change its value.
3. In a dialog box, only one option button can be active at one time.
4. Use the Close button to exit a dialog box.

THE WINDOWS CLIPBOARD

Windows contains an object called the **clipboard** that allows you to copy text or graphics from one application to another. The Windows clipboard is an area in memory that an application uses to store data temporarily during a cut, paste, or copy operation.

A Copy command occurs when a likeness of data is placed in the clipboard, leaving the original data unchanged. The Cut command removes the data from its original location and places it in the clipboard. The Paste command removes data from the clipboard and places it in a document.

The clipboard can only handle data from one Cut or Copy command. Data in the clipboard is destroyed and replaced when a subsequent Cut or Copy command is issued. Using a Paste command leaves the data in the clipboard unchanged. You will use the clipboard in the following Hands-On Exercise involving the Windows drawing program, Paint. Table 1.4 shows the tool box buttons that appear in the Paint window and what you can do with them.

Hands-On Exercise: Using the Paint Program

1. Start the Paint application.

Click the Start button. The Start menu appears.

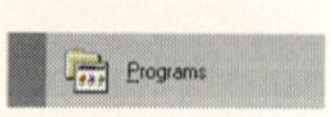

Point to this option to open the Programs menu.

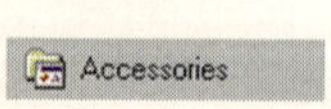

Point to this option to open the Accessories menu.

TIMELY TIP

If you make a mistake as you are working on this exercise, you can issue the Undo command by choosing Undo from the Edit menu. This command allows you to erase any mistakes.

Table 1.4 Paint Tool Box Buttons

Button	Name	Allows You To:
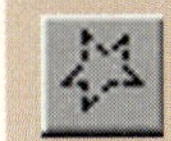	Free-Form Select	Select irregular-shaped areas of the image for a move, copy, or edit
	Select	Initiate a drag operation to select a rectangular area of the image for a move, copy, or edit
	Eraser/Color Eraser	Selectively erase parts of the image
	Fill With Color	Fill a delimited area with the selected color from the palette
	Pick Color	Select a colored area of an image to copy to another part of the image
	Magnifier	Enlarge an area of the image a selected amount
	Pencil	Draw a line one pixel (dot) wide
	Brush	Draw or create an image
	Airbrush	Airbrush the image
	Text	Label parts of the image
	Line	Draw a line of a selected thickness
	Curve	Draw a curve of a selected thickness
	Rectangle	Draw a rectangle with a selected fill style
	Polygon	Draw a polygon with a selected fill style
	Ellipse	Draw an ellipse with a selected fill style
	Rounded Rectangle	Draw a rounded rectangle with a selected fill style

Click to start the Paint program. If necessary, click the Maximize button to enlarge the Paint window. You should now see the application window shown in Figure 1.43. The tool box with its buttons appears on the left side of the window. You will now create the computer image shown in Figure 1.44.

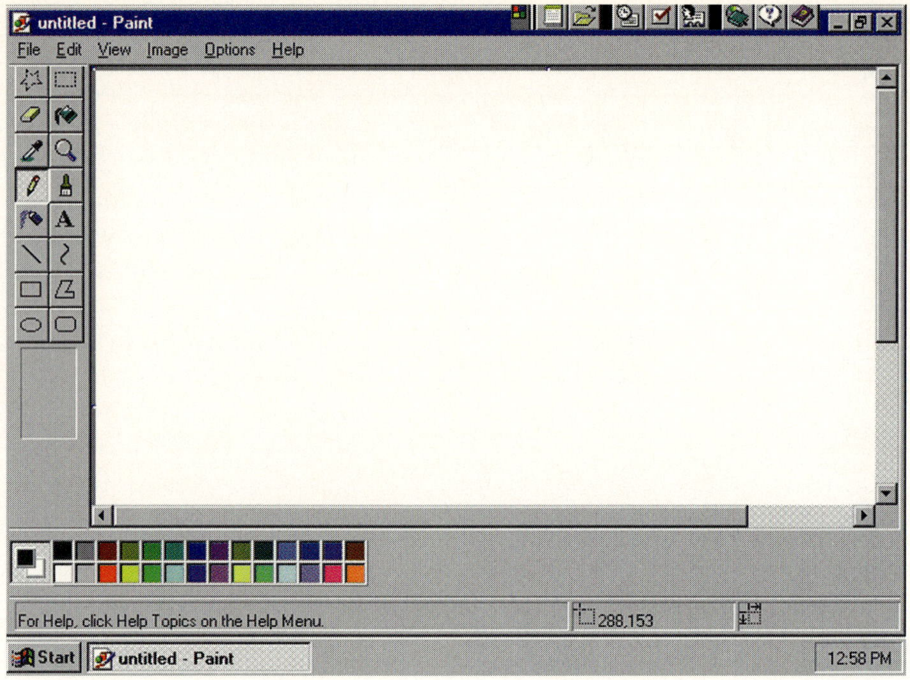

Figure 1.43
The application window for the Paint program.

2. Create the outside of the monitor shown in Figure 1.45.

Click to activate the Rectangle tool.

Click and drag — Click to anchor the upper-left corner of the monitor outline, and then drag down and to the right until the outline appears as shown in Figure 1.45.

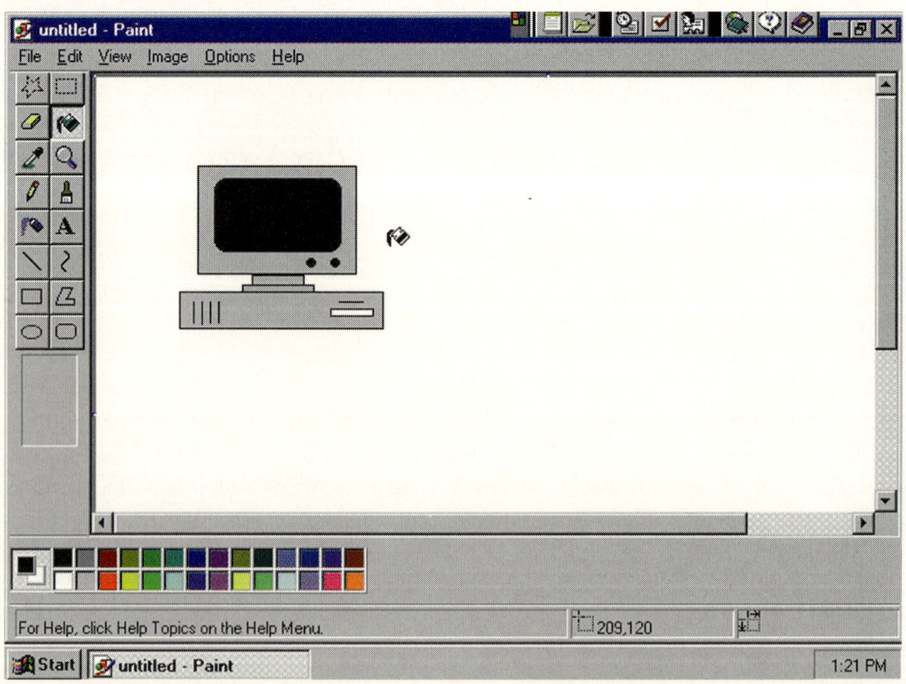

Figure 1.44
The computer image you will create in this exercise.

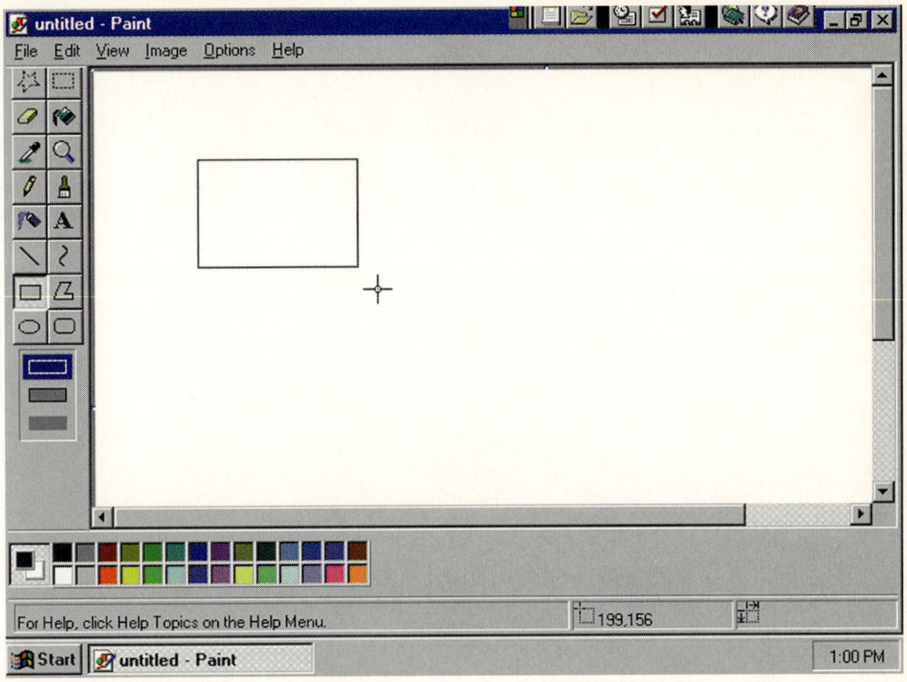

Figure 1.45
The outline of the monitor created by using the Rectangle button.

3. Create the screen of the monitor shown in Figure 1.46.

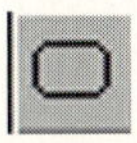

Click to activate the Rounded Rectangle tool.

Click and drag — Click to anchor the upper-left corner of the screen outline, and then drag down and to the right until the screen outline appears as shown in Figure 1.46.

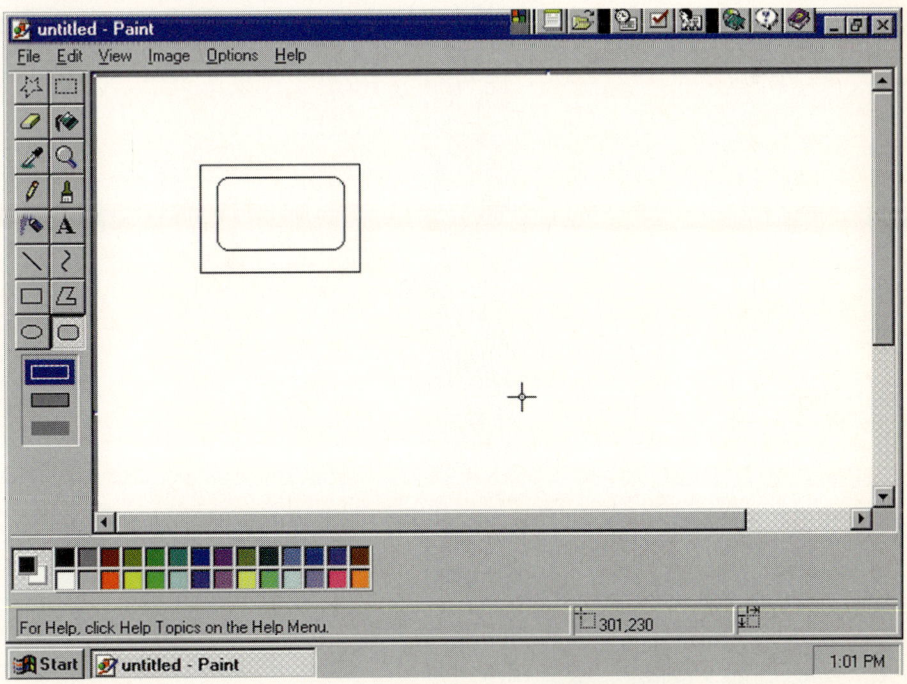

Figure 1.46
The outline of the monitor screen created by using the Rounded Rectangle button.

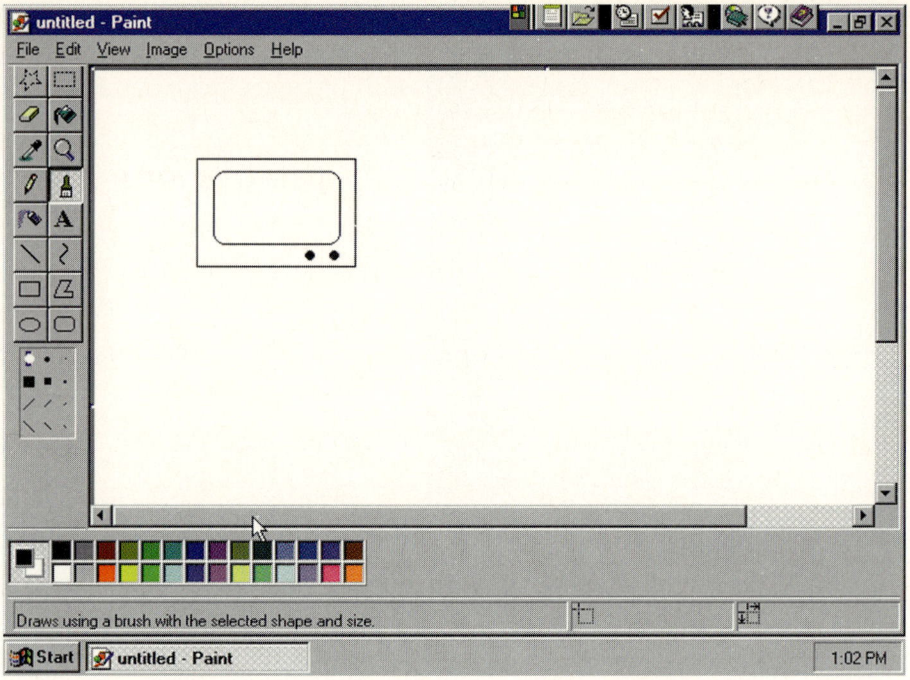

Figure 1.47
The brightness and contrast knobs added to the monitor.

4. **Draw the brightness and contrast knobs on the monitor shown in Figure 1.47.**

Click to activate the Brush tool.

Click on the first dot icon to activate this shape and size.

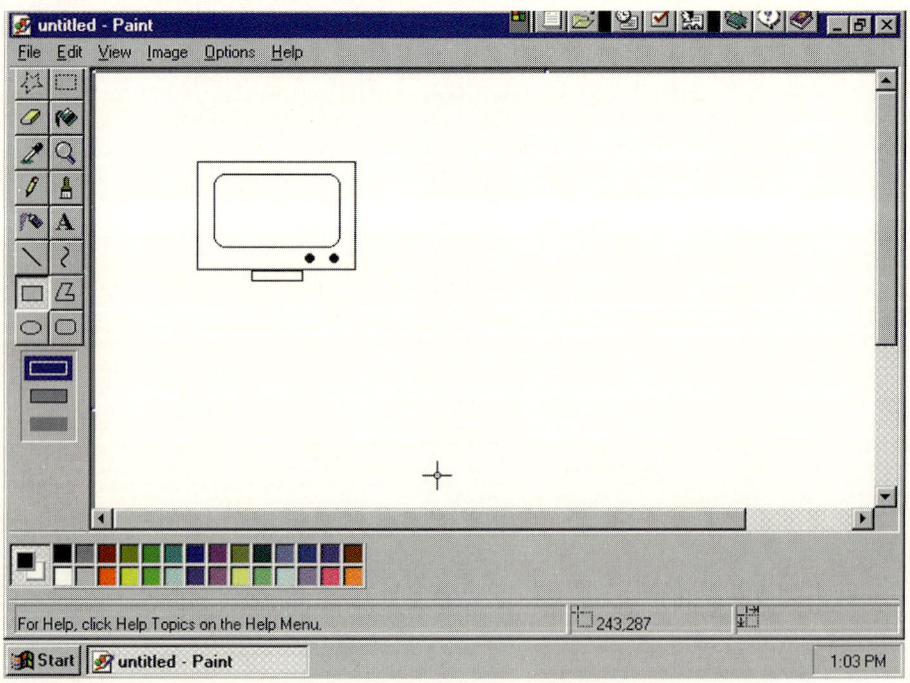

Figure 1.48
The stem of the monitor stand created by using the Rectangle button.

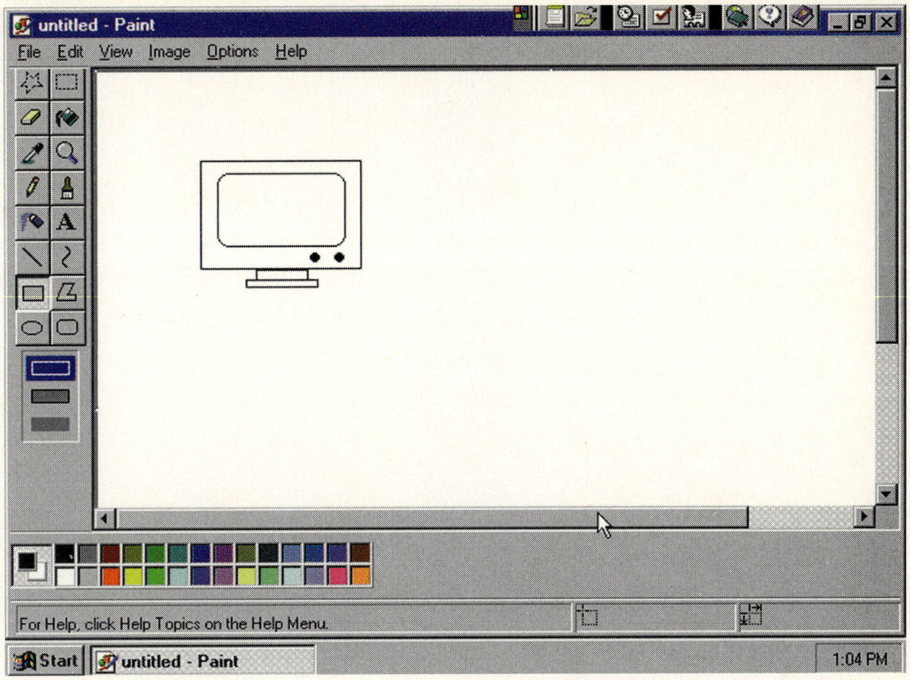

Figure 1.49
The base of the monitor created by using the Rectangle button.

Click — Click in the correct positions on the drawn monitor to draw the knobs shown in Figure 1.47.

5. **Create the stem of the monitor stand shown in Figure 1.48.**

 Click to activate the Rectangle tool.

Click and drag — Click to anchor the upper-left corner of the monitor stand stem, and then drag down and to the right until the stem appears as shown in Figure 1.48.

6. **Create the base of the monitor shown in Figure 1.49.**

Click and drag — Click to anchor the upper-left corner of the base outline, and then drag down and to the right until the base appears as shown in Figure 1.49.

7. **Create the system box beneath the monitor shown in Figure 1.50.**

Click and drag — Click to anchor the upper-left corner of the system box, and then drag down and to the right until the system box appears as shown in Figure 1.50.

8. **Draw the air vents and the $3^1/_2$-inch disk drive openings shown in Figure 1.51.**

 Click to activate the Line tool.

Click and drag — Click to anchor the top location of each vent, and then drag down to the ending location until the vertical vents appear as shown in Figure 1.51.

9. **Add the 3½-inch disk drive opening shown in Figure 1.52.**

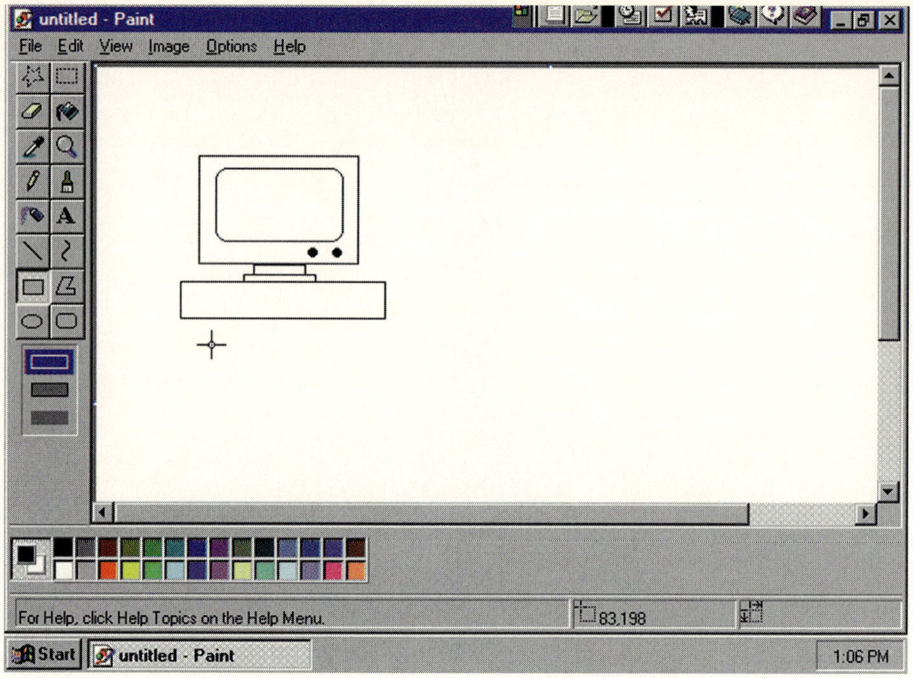

Figure 1.50
The outline of the system box created by using the Rectangle button.

Click and drag — Click to anchor the left location of the drive opening, and then drag it to the ending location until the horizontal opening appears as shown in Figure 1.52.

10. Add the CD-ROM drive shown in Figure 1.53.

 Click to activate the Rectangle feature.

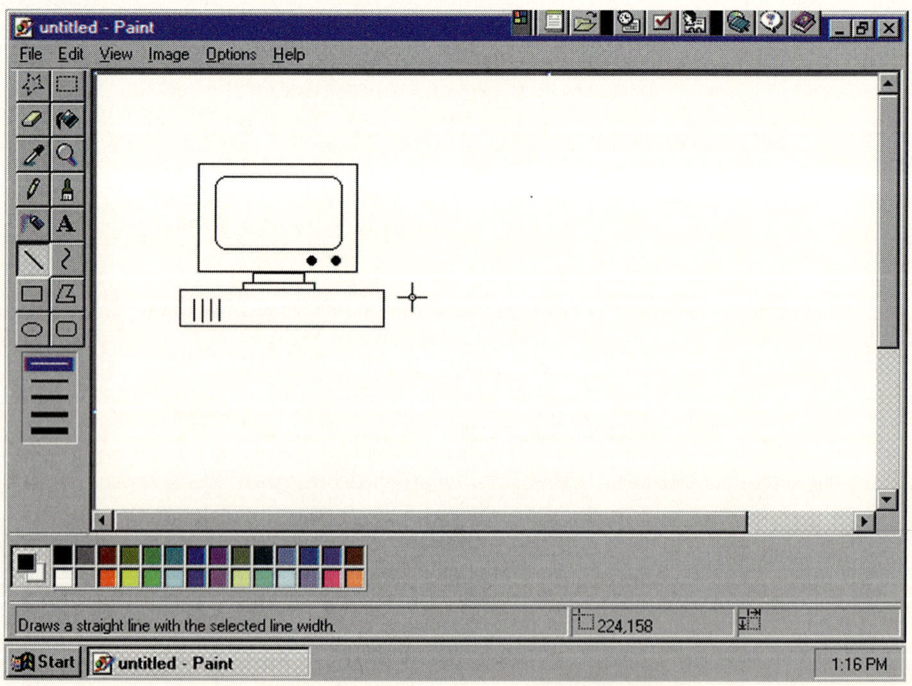

Figure 1.51
The system box with the vertical vents added.

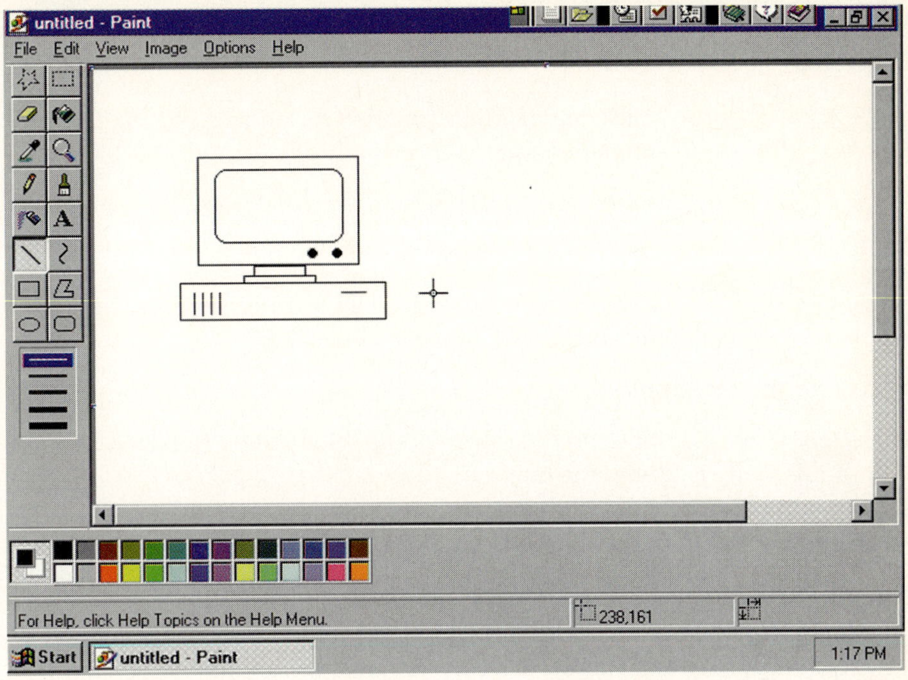

Figure 1.52
The system box with the disk drive opening added.

Click and drag — Click to anchor the upper-left corner of the CD-ROM drive outline, and then drag down and to the right until the drive outline appears as shown in Figure 1.53.

11. Color the system components light gray.

 Click this square of the color palette.

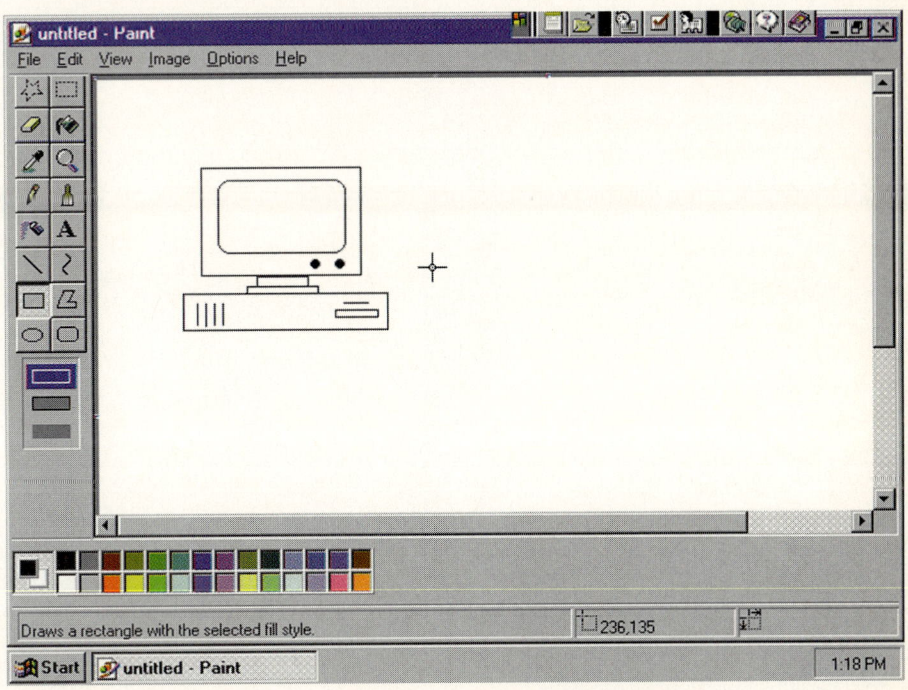

Figure 1.53
The CD-ROM drive added to the system box.

	Click to activate the Fill With Color tool.
Click	Click outside of the rounded rectangle screen to color the monitor frame.
Click	Click the stem of the monitor to color it.
Click	Click the base of the monitor to color it.
Click	Click the system box to color it. Your computer should now appear as shown in Figure 1.54.

12. Color the screen black.

	Click on this square of the color palette (top row, first from the left).
Click	Click inside the rounded rectangle screen to color the screen. Your finished computer should now appear as shown in Figure 1.55.

13. Copy the finished computer to the Windows clipboard.

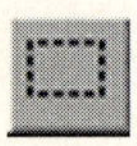	Click to activate the Select feature.
Click and drag	Place a selection rectangle around the finished computer. Your screen should now look like Figure 1.56.
Edit	Select this option from the menu bar to open the Edit menu.

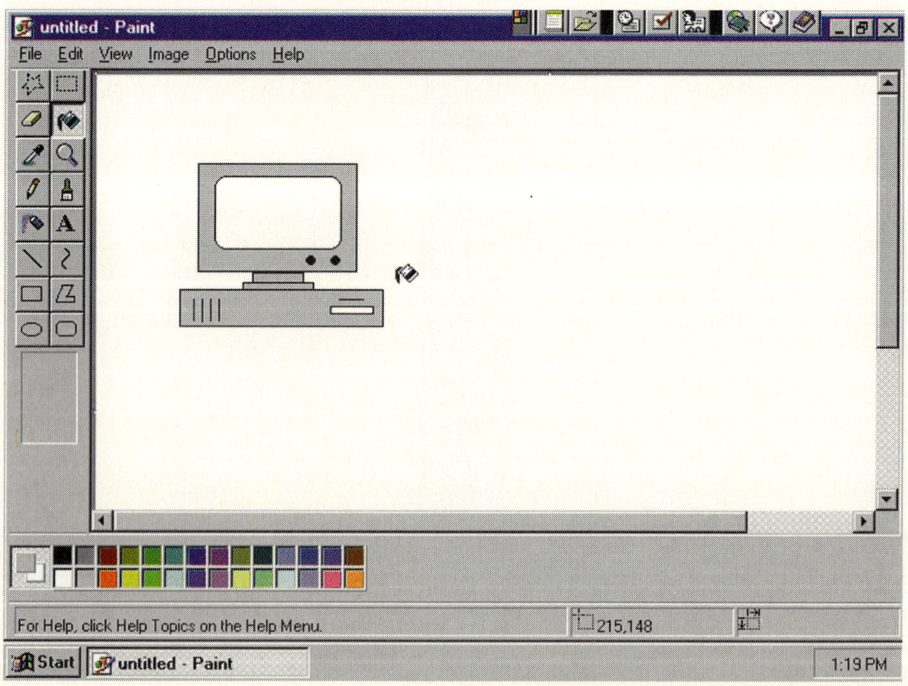

Figure 1.54
The system components colored gray.

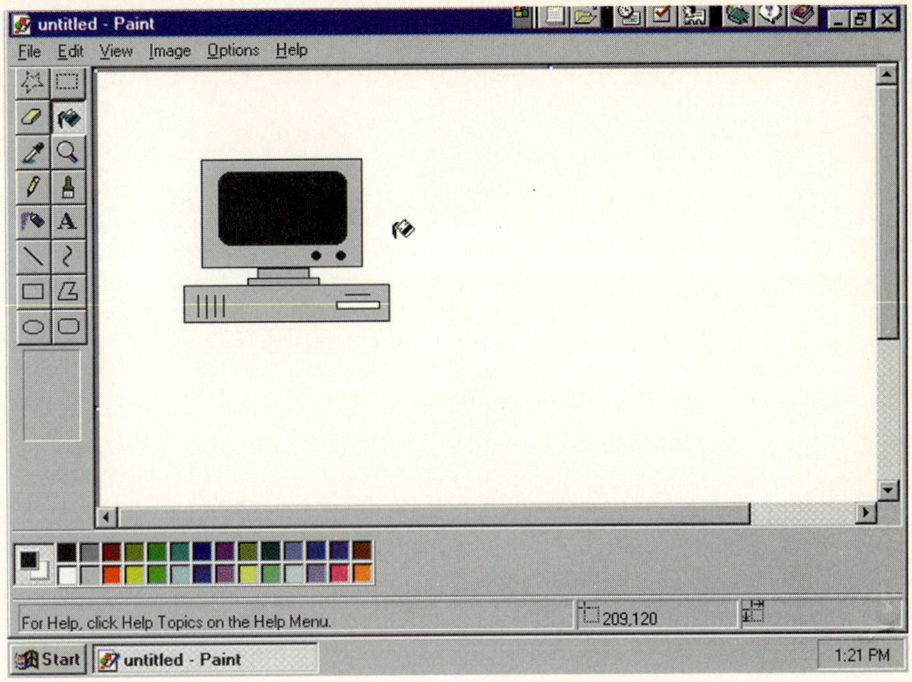

Figure 1.55
The finished computer with a black screen.

Copy Select this option from the Edit menu to copy the contents of the selection to the Windows clipboard.

14. **Paste a copy of the computer drawing.**

Edit Select this option from the menu bar to open the Edit menu.

Paste Select this option to place a copy of the computer in the upper-left corner of the screen.

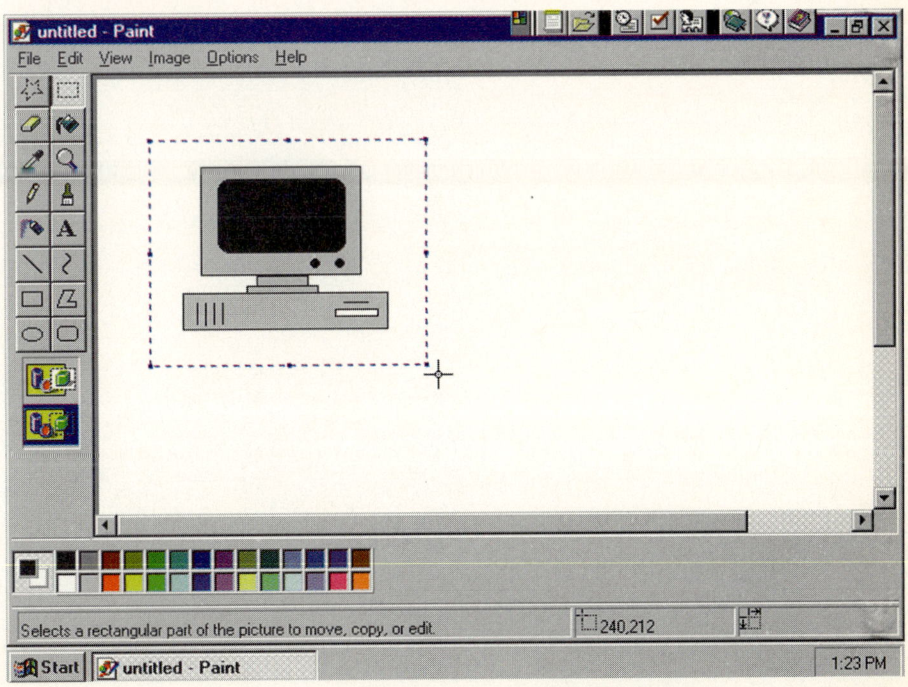

Figure 1.56
The selected computer drawing.

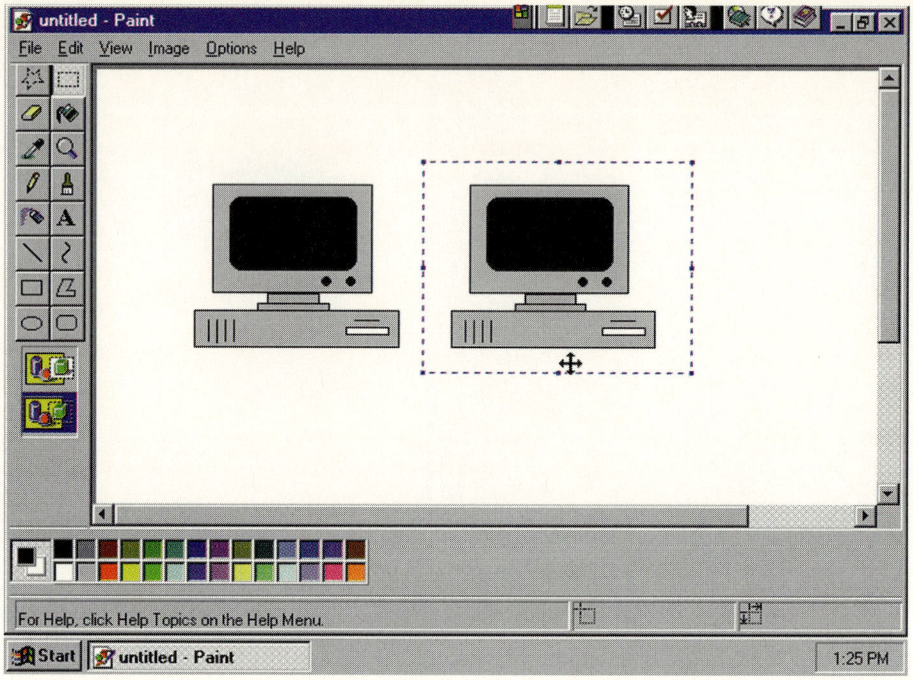

Figure 1.57
The copied computer placed next to the original computer drawing.

Click and drag	Move the copied computer drawing to the location shown in Figure 1.57 by dragging the selection.
Click	Click anywhere outside the drawing to cancel the selection.

15. Print the drawing.

File	Click to open the File menu.
Print. . .	Click to open the Print dialog box shown in Figure 1.58.

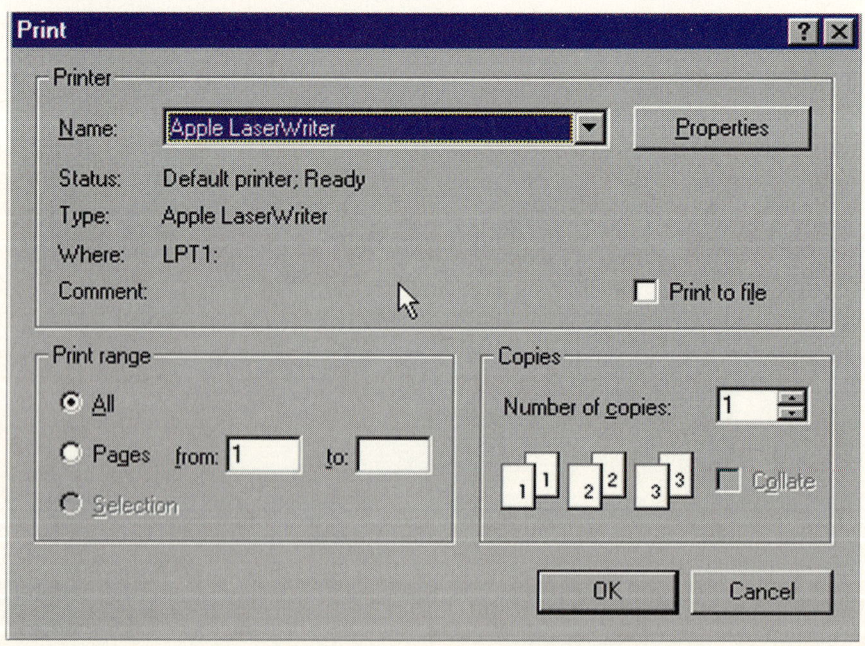

Figure 1.58
The Print dialog box of Paint.

Print the drawing.

16. Return to the desktop.

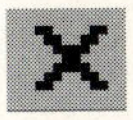

Click the Close button. Paint asks if you want to save the changes.

Click the "No" command button to exit without saving the drawings.

On Your Own

- Start four application programs that appear in the Programs menu.
- If the application opens in a full screen, click the Restore button as you start each program.
- Move the application windows so that a part of each is visible.
- Move from one application to another by clicking on a part of that application window.
- Move from one application to another by clicking on that application's taskbar button.

Reinforcing the Exercise

1. Using the tools from the Paint tool box, you can draw and color a wide variety of images.
2. Before you can copy an object, you must select that object.
3. You use the Edit, Paste command sequence to place a copy of an object in a Paint window.

ACCESSING THE WINDOWS HELP FEATURE

The Windows **Help feature** provides several different types of help. You can access help by using Tooltips, the What's this button, the Help option of the Start menu, or ScreenTips.

Using ToolTips

A **ToolTip** is a small text box that appears when you position the pointer on a control.

TIMELY TIP

If you don't want to use the mouse, you can access help in most Windows applications or dialog boxes by pressing the (F1) function key.

Using the What's this Button

The What's this button contains a question mark (?) and usually appears at the top of the open window or dialog box. If there is no What's this button displayed, look for a Help command button.

Once you click the What's this button, a question mark appears to the right of the pointer, indicating that you are in Help mode. When you click an item in the window or dialog box, a **ScreenTip** appears with a description about the control that you clicked.

TIMELY TIP

You can also activate a ScreenTip by right-clicking the object you need information about. A context menu appears, and you choose What's this? to display a ScreenTip.

Using the Start Button

You access Windows' primary Help feature by choosing Help from the Start menu. Invoking the Help command in this way opens the Help Topics dialog box, which is composed of three tabs: Context, Index, and Find.

Hands-On Exercise: Using the Windows Help Feature

1. **Examine a ToolTip.**

11:22 AM — Point to the time in the status bar, and let the pointer stay there until a ToolTip with the day and date appears (Figure 1.59).

Figure 1.59
A ToolTip displayed for the clock icon of the Windows taskbar.

2. **Examine a ScreenTip in a dialog box.**

Double-click the My Computer icon to open that window.

View — Click to open the View menu.

Options. . . — Click to open the Options dialog box.

O Browse folders by using — Right-click the second entry in the dialog box, which starts with this text. A context menu with only the What's this? entry appears.

What's this? — Click to display the ScreenTip for this entry (Figure 1.60).

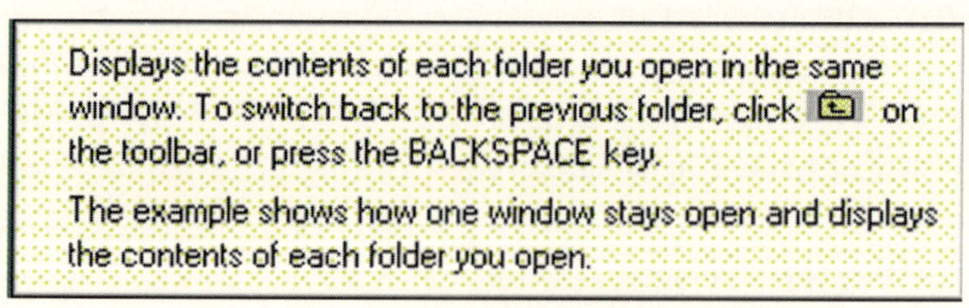

Figure 1.60
The ScreenTip for the second Browse button of the Folder tab of the Options dialog box.

Click — Click in any unused area of the window if necessary to close the ScreenTip.

Click Cancel to close the Options dialog box.

Click Close to close the My Computer window.

3. Open the Help dialog box.

Click to display the Start menu.

Click to display the Help Topics dialog box (Figure 1.61). The Contents tab should be displayed. If it isn't, click that tab to activate it. In the displayed list, each book icon represents a topic that, when selected will generate a new list of topics.

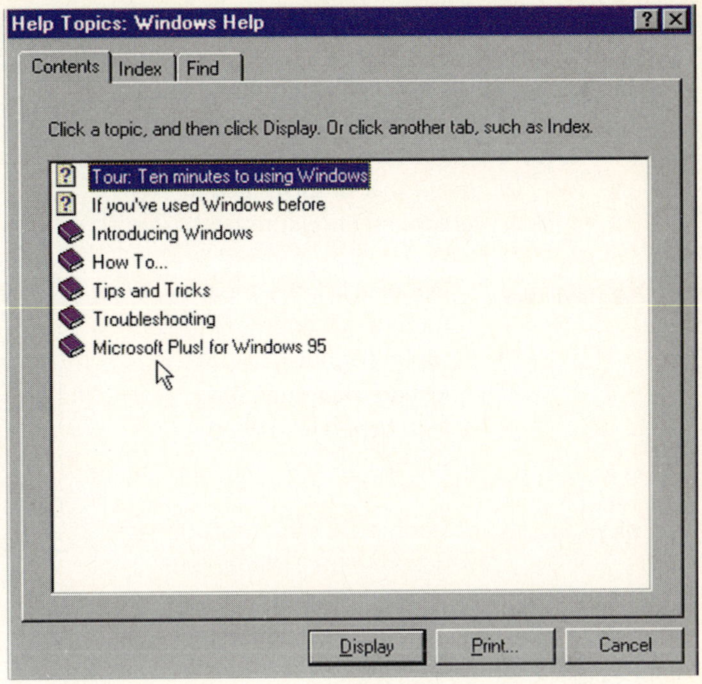

Figure 1.61
The Help Topics dialog box with three tabs.

4. Use the What's this button at the top of the dialog box.

Click to add a large black question mark to the right of the pointer.

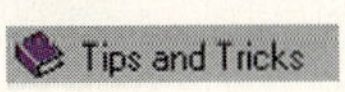

Click to display the ScreenTip for this entry (Figure 1.62).

Click — Click an unused area of the desktop to close the ScreenTip.

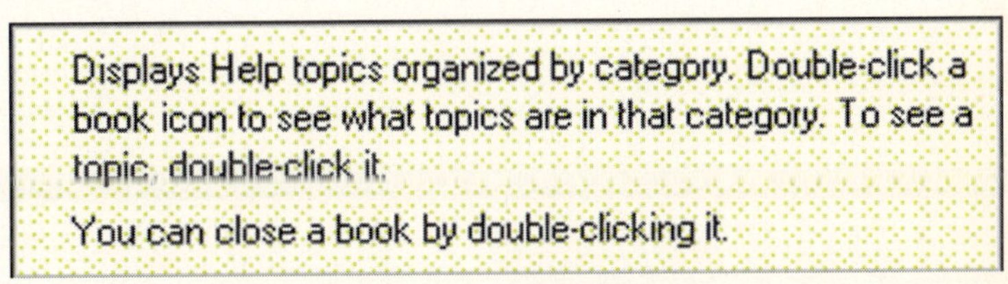

Figure 1.62
The ScreenTip generated when you click the What's this button in the Help Topics dialog box and then check the How To. . . entry.

5. Use the Contents tab to obtain help.

How To... — Double-click this topic. The book icon changes to an open book, and a number of topics appear beneath it (Figure 1.63).

Run Programs — Double-click this topic to generate another list of topics (Figure 1.64). Selecting a question mark icon generates a Help screen.

Run Programs — Double-click this topic to generate the Help screen shown in Figure 1.65.

Options... — Click to display the Options menu.

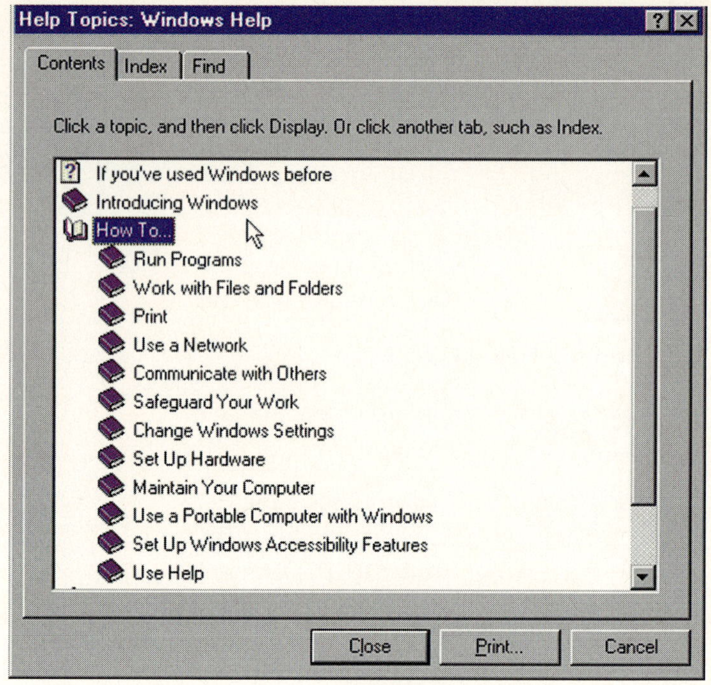

Figure 1.63
The topics displayed by selecting the How To topic.

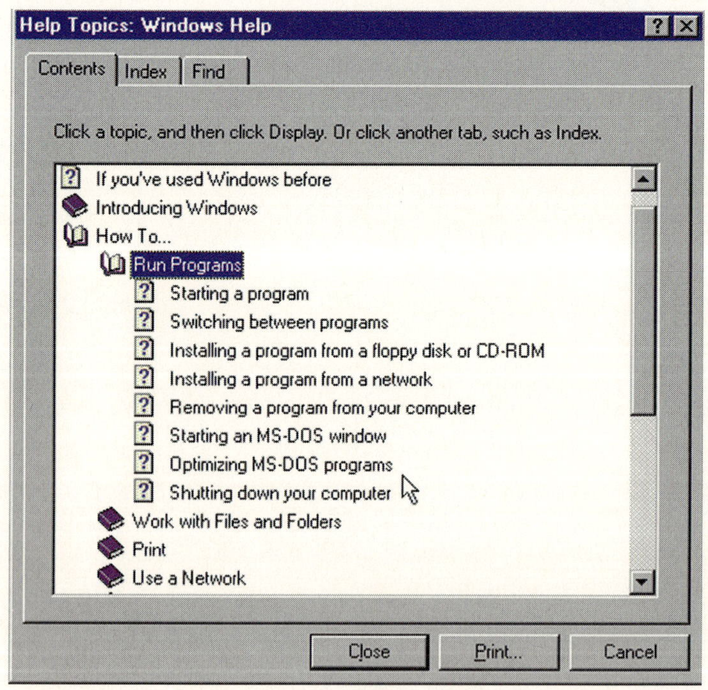

Figure 1.64
The topics displayed by selecting the Run Programs Help topic.

Print Topic. . . Click to open the Print dialog box.

OK Click to print the text from the Help window.

Help Topics Click to return to the Help Topics dialog box.

Shutting down your computer Click this topic.

Display Click to display the Help screen shown in Figure 1.66.

Options... Click to open the Options menu.

Copy Click to copy the text in this window to the clipboard.

Help Topics Click this button to return to the Help Topics dialog box.

6. Access help for pop-up messages using the Index tab.

Index Activate the Index tab (Figure 1.67).

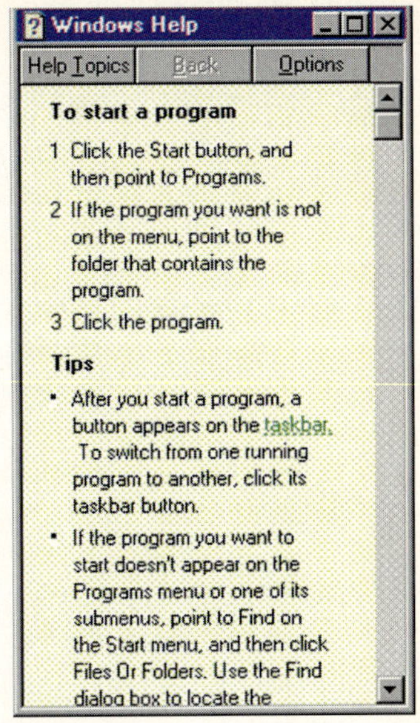

Figure 1.65
The Starting a Program Help screen.

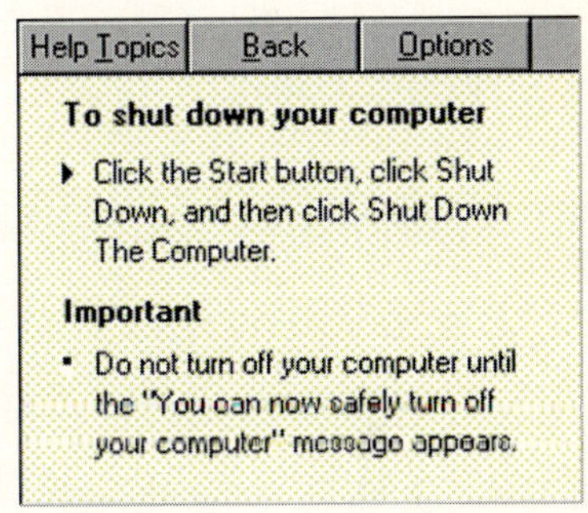

Figure 1.66
The Help screen displayed for the Shutting down your computer option.

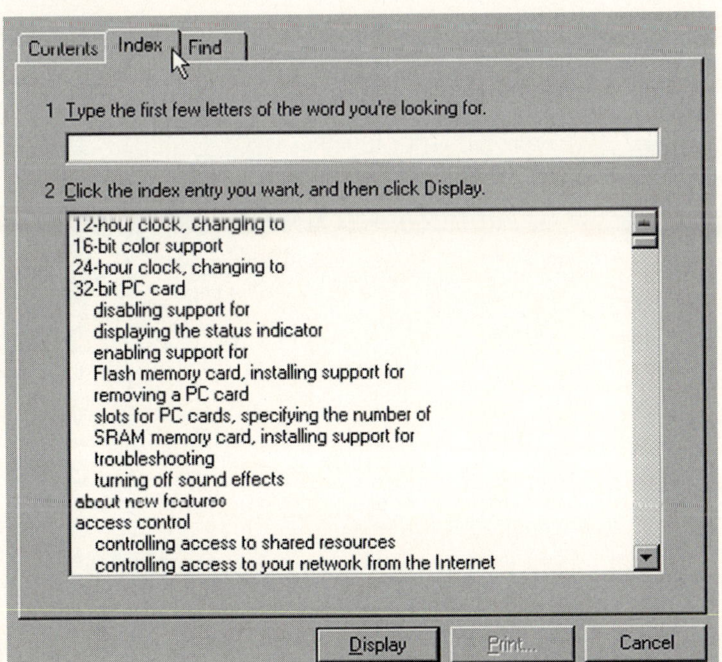

Figure 1.67
The Index tab provides a search feature that locates the topic you want.

Type: **pop-up**	Enter this text in the text box at the top of the Index tab. A list of related topics appears in the lower list box (Figure 1.68).
pop-up messages	Double-click this topic to display the Help screen shown in Figure 1.69.
	Click to exit Help.

7. **WordPad is Window's built-in word processor.** Open the WordPad program, and look at the text you copied to the clipboard.

	Click to open the Start menu.
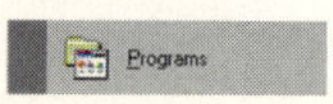	Open the Programs menu.
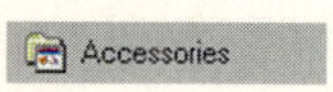	Open the Accessories menu.

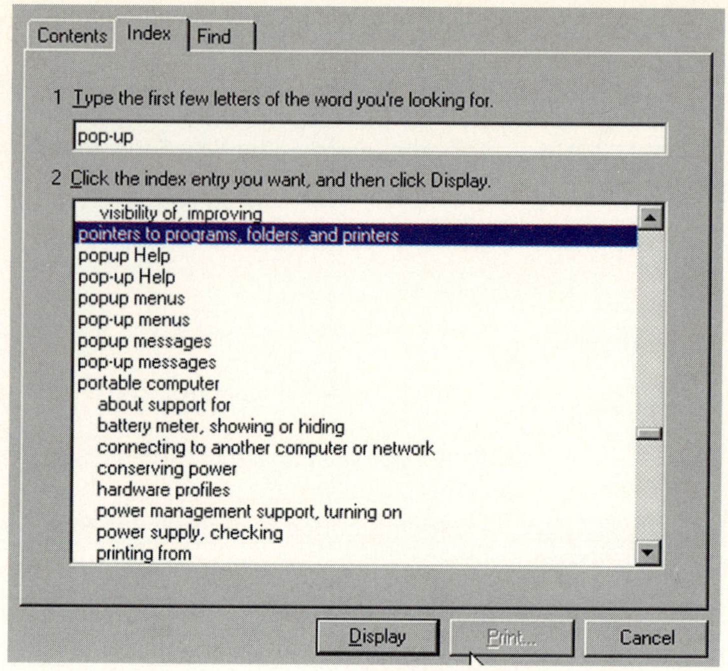

Figure 1.68
The matching Help topics located for the *pop-up* topic.

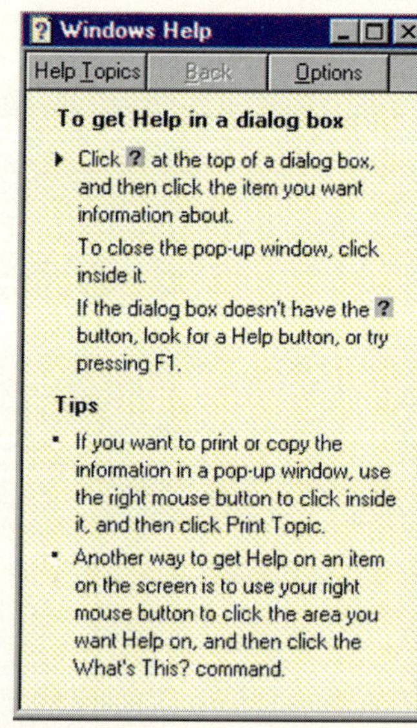

Figure 1.69
The Help screen for the *pop-up messages* topic.

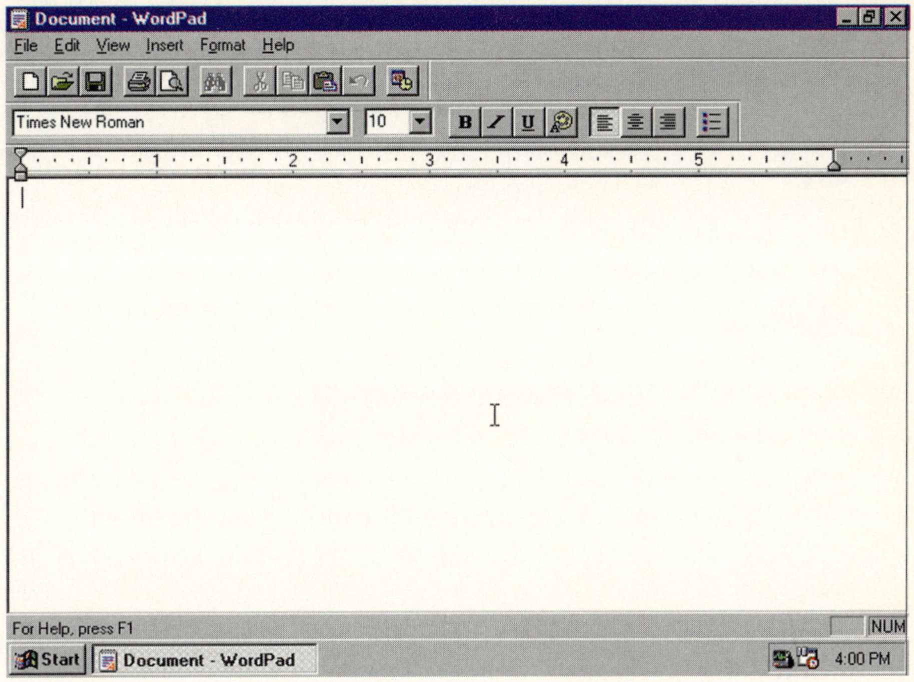

Figure 1.70
The WordPad application window.

Click to start WordPad. The window shown in Figure 1.70 appears.

Edit Open the Edit pull-down menu.

Paste Click to copy the text from the clipboard. The WordPad window should now look like Figure 1.71. The text appears on-screen exactly as it will print to paper. This is referred to as "what you see is what you get" or **WYSIWYG.**

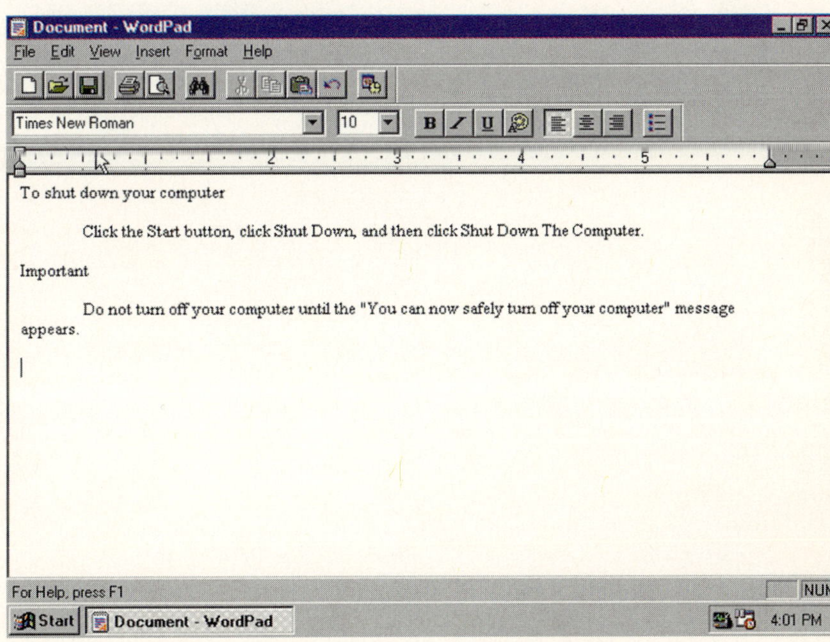

Figure 1.71
The text from the clipboard as it appears in the WordPad window.

Click to print the document. Your printed page should look exactly like the document on-screen.

Click to return to the Windows desktop. WordPad now displays a dialog box that asks if you want to save changes to the document (Figure 1.72).

Click to return to the desktop without saving changes.

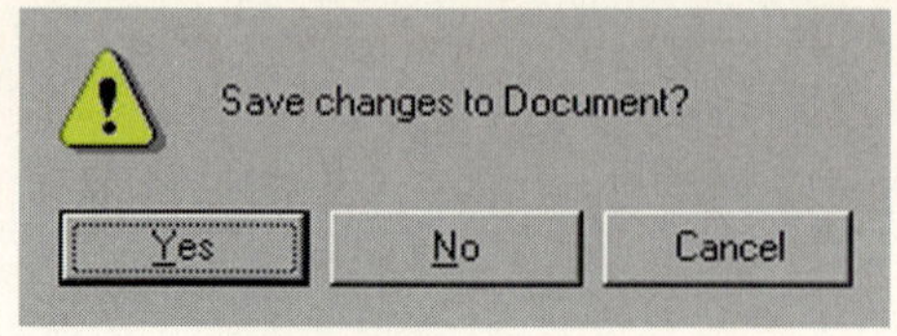

Figure 1.72
The WordPad dialog box prompting you about saving any changes.

Reinforcing the Exercise

1. When you point to an object and allow the pointer to remain on the object for a short time, a ToolTip appears, displaying information about that object.
2. When you click the What's this button, a question mark appears on the right side of the pointer.
3. You can open a ScreenTip by right-clicking the object you need information on and then choosing What's this? from the context menu.
4. The Help Topics dialog box has three tabs: Context, Index, and Find.

On Your Own

- Issue the Start, Programs, Accessories, Games command sequence.
- Open Solitaire and play one game.
- Issue the Start, Programs, Accessories command sequence, and start WordPad. Enter a short note and print it. Examine the various menu commands available. Try out some of the commands.

SESSION REVIEW

Windows 95 automatically starts when you turn on your computer. If your computer is connected to a network, you may have to log onto the network via a Windows dialog box.

Windows uses a graphic user interface (GUI) that allows you to enter commands easily, either by using a mouse as a pointing tool or by entering commands from the keyboard. Once you start Windows, you invoke commands by using objects from the desktop. The desktop may contain more than one window. The active window is on top with a colored title bar. Some commands may also require you to enter some additional information in dialog boxes.

The Windows interface uses graphic images called icons to represent applications or objects. Using the Minimize button, you can also reduce an application to a button on the taskbar. To reopen the application, you click on its taskbar button.

Application windows can be either active or inactive. An active window is the top window with the colored title bar; any other windows are inactive. Only an active window can have commands executed in it. An inactive window can be activated by clicking on any part of that window or clicking its corresponding button in the taskbar.

You can resize any window by using the Maximize, Minimize, and Restore buttons. You can also resize them by using the mouse to drag window borders. The pointer changes shape to show the direction of the resizing operation.

The easiest way to close a window is by clicking the Close button on the title bar. You also can close a window by double-clicking the control-menu button.

Windows makes extensive use of menus. Menu options represent commands. When you select an option on the menu bar, a pull-down menu appears with more options to choose from. Many commands, called shortcut commands, can also be executed by using the keyboard rather than a menu.

You can access the Help feature of Windows by choosing Help from the Start menu or by using ToolTips, ScreenTips, or the What's this button. You can also copy information from Help screens into the Windows clipboard and print the information.

KEY TERMS AND CONCEPTS

active window 1–8
border 1–13
click 1–3
clipboard 1–26
Close button 1–15
controls 1–21
command sequence 1–18
deselect 1–3
desktop 1–2
dialog box 1–21
disk operating system (DOS) 1–1
double-click 1–3
drag 1–3
graphic user interface (GUI) 1–1
Help feature 1–37
icon 1–3
inactive window 1–8
menu bar 1–18
mouse 1–1
multitasking 1–8
object 1–3
operating system 1–1
point 1–3
pop-up messages 1–42
property 1–3
pull-down menu 1–18
resize a window 1–13
right-click 1–3
ScreenTip 1–38
scroll bar 1–15
scroll box 1–15
shortcut command 1–18
size grip 1–13
status bar 1–19
taskbar 1–7
title bar 1–14
Tooltip 1–37
WYSIWYG 1–43

SESSION QUIZ

Multiple Choice

1. Which of the following objects provides information about your computer's resources?
   a. inbox
   b. taskbar
   c. My Computer
   d. Network Neighborhood
2. What is the term used by Windows to indicate the whole screen?
   a. macro window
   b. dialog box
   c. desktop
   d. active window
3. Which of the following buttons can reduce an application to a button on the taskbar?
   a. Maximize
   b. control-menu
   c. Minimize
   d. Restore
4. The process of having multiple applications available for use at one time is called:
   a. windowing
   b. multitasking
   c. multiprocessing
   d. multiple windows
5. Which of the following statement(s) about the Help feature is (are) true?
   a. You can activate the Help feature by pressing the F1 key.
   b. Clicking the What's this button changes the appearance of the pointer.
   c. The Help feature allows you to copy text from Help screens to the clipboard.
   d. You cannot look up information about a specific topic using the Help feature.

True/False

6. A window that resides beneath another window is an active window.
7. You can enter Windows commands only by using a mouse or trackball.
8. You can activate a minimized application by clicking that application's button on the taskbar.
9. Clicking and dragging the title bar of a window resizes that window.
10. The Windows pointer changes shape depending on the task being performed.

SESSION REVIEW EXERCISES

1. Define or describe each of the following:
   a. My Computer
   b. active window
   c. desktop
   d. taskbar
   e. clipboard
2. A shortcut or context menu can be activated by clicking the ______________ button of the mouse.
3. In a window or dialog box, a button with question mark on it is known as the ______________ ______________ button.
4. The ______________ ______________ icon opens a window that allows you to examine the available computer resources.
5. The acronym GUI means ______________ ______________ ______________.
6. The pointing device most frequently used with Windows is the ______________.
7. The entire Windows screen is called the ______________.
8. Pressing and releasing the mouse button is called ______________.
9. Holding down the mouse button and moving the mouse is called ______________.
10. The ______________ button on the taskbar opens a menu that can lead you through a whole series of menus.
11. Allowing the pointer to rest over an icon displays a ______________ explaining that icon's function.
12. The ______________ button is used to shrink an application window to a button on the taskbar.
13. Clicking the ______________ button closes an application window.
14. An ______________ after a pull-down menu option indicates that if this command is selected a dialog box will appear on the screen.
15. The ______________ button changes a maximized window back to its original size.
16. The ______________ bar is used to move quickly through text or information contained in a window.
17. The ______________ acts as a temporary storage area to allow you to copy information or graphic images from one application to another.
18. The active window is always the ______________ window on the screen.
19. Pressing the ______________ key activates the Help feature of Windows.
20. When you click a *What's this* button in a dialog box and then click an object in the dialog box, a ______________ opens with information about that object.

COMPUTER EXERCISES

1. Practice using the mouse.
   a. Click the Start button, and then open the Programs and Accessories menus.
   b. Select the game Solitaire.
   c. Play one game of Solitaire to practice clicking and dragging.
   d. Close the Solitaire window.
2. Practice opening and closing Windows applications.
   a. Start and exit two or three Windows applications. Be sure to use the Close button, or choose Exit from the File option of the menu bar to close an application.
   b. Close any application window when you are finished.
   c. Open Excel. Click its Restore button. Open Word. Click its Restore button. You should now have a screen that looks something like Figure 1.73. Maximize the first window and close it using the Close button. Do the same for the remaining window.
3. Practice using the Windows Help feature.
   a. Double-click the time in the taskbar to open the Date/Time Properties dialog box.
   b. Right-click the clock, and then click the What's this? menu entry. A ScreenTip now appears. Click anywhere to make the text box disappear.
   c. Click on the calendar portion of the dialog box. Press the (F1) key and a Help text box appears for the calendar. Click anywhere to make the text box disappear.
   d. Click the What's this icon at the top of the Date/Time Properties dialog box. A question mark now appears beside the pointer. Click the OK button at the bottom of the dialog box. A Help text box appears. Click the Cancel button to close the Date/Time Properties dialog box.

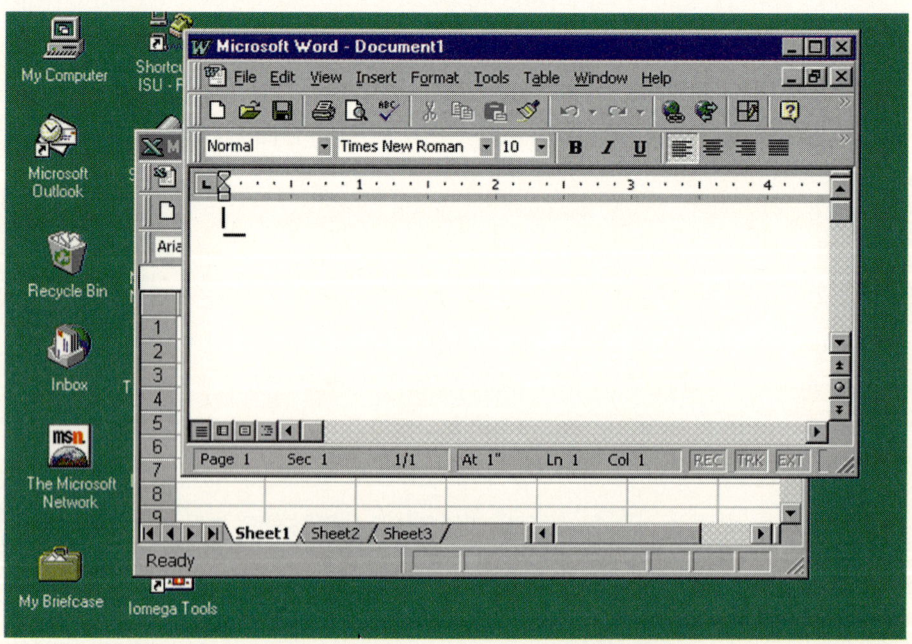

Figure 1.73
The Windows desktop with the Excel and Word windows both visible.

e. Activate the Help feature by using the Start button. Click the Index tab. Type the word *date*. Double-click the entry in the selection box that contains *daylight saving time, adjusting clock for*. Open the Options menu and select the Print Topic command. Click the OK button in the Print dialog box. Click the Cancel button to close the Help Topics dialog box.

4. Practice changing the size of the My Computer window.
   a. Minimize the My Computer window.
   b. Open the My Computer window.
   c. Maximize the My Computer window.
   d. Restore the My Computer window to its previous size.
5. Practice activating and using various accessory programs.
   a. Click the Start button, and point to Programs and then Accessories. From the Accessories menu, activate the Paint program. Using the mouse and the various icons along the left and bottom borders, experiment with the Paint application. Minimize the Paint window to a taskbar icon.
   c. Activate the Calculator from the Accessories menu.
      1) Perform the following calculations:
         1945/23=______
         125*453=______
         128+234+287+765=__________
      2) Reduce the Calculator to a taskbar button.
   d. Activate the Paint program by using its taskbar button.
   e. Activate the Calculator program by using its taskbar button.
   f. Click the Close button of the Calculator window to close it.
   g. Click the Close button of the Paint window to close it. Answer No when requested about saving any changes.

SESSION 2

Manipulating Documents and Folders

After completing this session, you should be able to:

- Distinguish between folders and documents
- Select multiple documents and folders
- Name, rename, delete, and copy documents and folders
- Create a folder
- Print a document
- Use the Print Manager
- Format a disk
- Use Windows Explorer

STORAGE OBJECTS

Windows 95 provides many different commands that allow you to interact with objects that you have saved to disk. This process of interaction is called **file maintenance.** To make its file maintenance system easy to understand, Windows uses a **folder** metaphor, which refers to the standard manila folder that holds one or more documents for storage in a filing cabinet.

In Windows' metaphorical folder, each piece of paper, or **document,** represents stored data that can be processed by an application program or by the computer itself. The folder is in a unique location on a disk. A disk can contain many different folders, and a folder can contain other folders as well as documents. Folders can hold such things as parts of the operating system, word processing documents, workbooks for use by a spreadsheet, and databases.

A document is similar to a **file** but file is a computer term rather than a windows-related term. Windows generally uses the term *document.*

Folders and Documents

A folder is represented by a manila folder icon whenever you have information about a disk drive displayed on-screen (Figure 2.1). You can display the contents of a drive, with its folders and documents (files), by double-clicking the icon for that drive in the My Computer window. You can then open a folder by double-clicking it.

Once a folder is open, any other folders or documents that it contains are displayed in a window (Figure 2.2). A document appears as a sheet of paper with an icon that indicates what type of information is stored in it. For instance, a Word document is represented by a sheet of paper with a big *W* toward the top of the page. A workbook file that was created by Excel appears with a large *X*. If Windows does not know what type of application program was used to create the document, it displays the Microsoft flag as the icon for that folder.

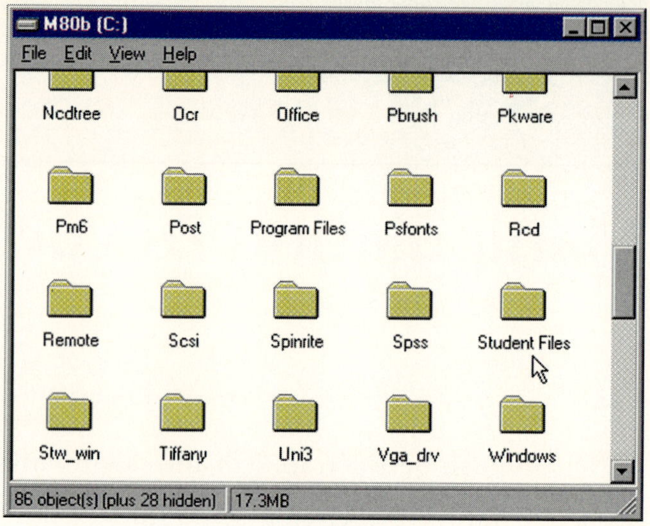

Figure 2.1
The drive C window with several folders visible. Your window may look dramatically different from this. For instance, you may have different software folders visible on your screen.

Naming a Folder or Document

When you name a folder or document, you want to generate a label that makes it easier to remember what's inside that folder or document. With Windows 95, you can use up to 255 characters, including spaces, in a folder or document name. This ability allows you to develop descriptive names more easily than you could with older versions of Windows or DOS.

Associating Documents with Applications

In a window like the one shown in Figure 2.2, a document with an application's logo as part of its icon is referred to as an associated document. An **associated document** has been saved to disk by a specific software application. If you double-click the icon for an associated document, the software application that was used to create that document is started and the document is loaded.

If you try to open a document that Windows has not associated with an application, Windows

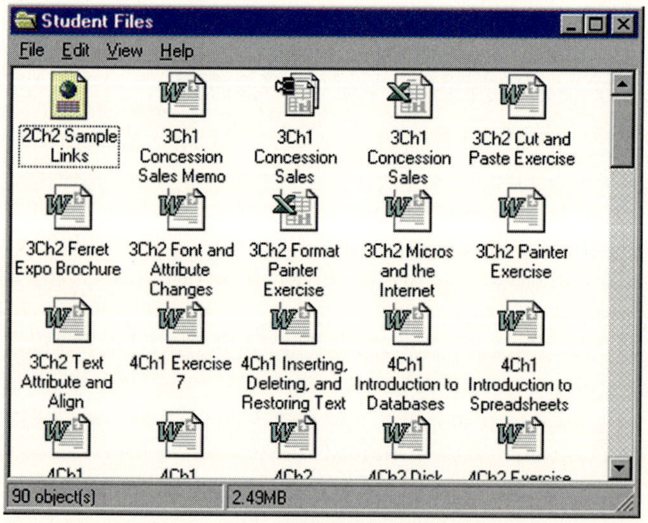

Figure 2.2
The Student Files folder opened with several different types of files displayed. This folder was created for storing files related to this textbook.

displays an Open With dialog box like that shown in Figure 2.3. You must then scroll through the list box and double-click the application program that is to be used with the selected document.

TIMELY TIP

> As you explore the various features of Windows, you may be working directly with documents. In such a situation, Windows may temporarily truncate long document names and end them with a tilde (~). This convention allows Windows 95 to retain compatibility with older versions of Windows and DOS. When you return to the desktop of Windows, the longer names will be displayed.

Selecting Documents and Folders

To select a document, folder, or multiple documents or folders, you use the mouse. Remember that folders and documents can both be referred to as objects.

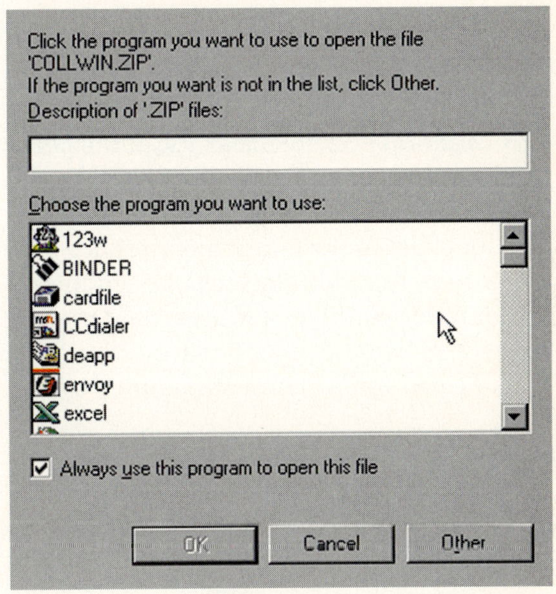

Figure 2.3
The Open With dialog box that appears when Windows does not know what application has been associated with a document.

Selecting a Single Object

To select a single object that you want to work with, you click the icon that represents that object. The color of the document or folder icon changes to blue (or some other color). Once you have selected the correct object, you can issue a command and begin working with it.

Selecting Adjacent Objects

You can **select adjacent objects** (documents or folders) in one of two ways: using SHIFT or using a drag operation. To use SHIFT, you select the first object by clicking it, hold down SHIFT, and then click the last object. All objects between the two selected objects are included in the selection and appear in blue.

To select multiple objects by using a drag operation, position the pointer to the left of the first object, and then click and drag to include the last object. As you drag the pointer, a rectangle forms around the objects, and the objects turn blue (Figure 2.4). When the rectangle encloses all the objects you want to select, release the left mouse button. The rectangle disappears, but the objects remain blue to indicate that they are selected. If you find that you have included the wrong objects in the selec-

TIMELY TIP

> Make certain that you do not begin a drag operation by positioning the pointer directly on the document or folder icon and clicking. If you do, you will be moving the object instead of including it in a selection. When such a mistake happens, just move the icon back to its original location. You can then click to the left of the icon to include it in the selection and complete the drag operation.

tion, you can cancel that selection by clicking any unused area of the window. Once you have the desired objects in the selection, you can issue a command.

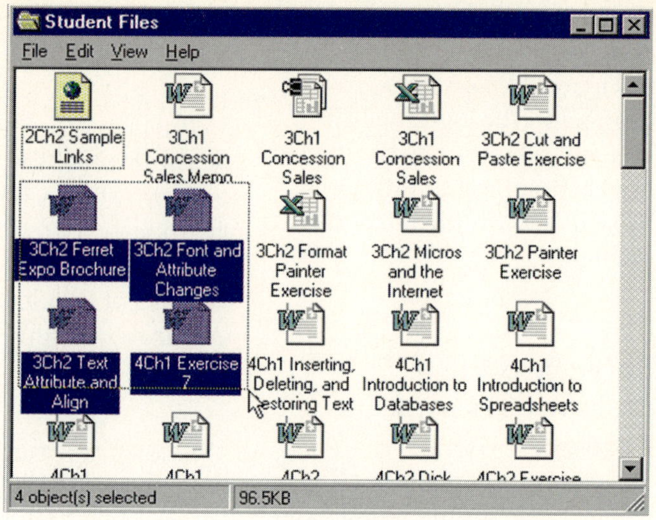

Figure 2.4
When you are using a drag operation to select multiple objects, a rectangle appears around the objects included in the selection.

Selecting Nonadjacent Objects

To **select nonadjacent objects,** you hold down (CTRL) as you click the icons of the documents and folders that you want to operate on.

Hands-On Exercise: Manipulating Disk Objects

This hands-on exercise makes use of the documents that are used with this text. If your documents reside on a disk in drive A, follow the steps indicated in Step 1; otherwise, use the steps indicated by your instructor to get to the location of the documents to be used with this text. If your files do not reside on drive A, make certain that you write down the procedure to access those files so you will have it for future use.

Figure 2.5
The Confirm File Delete dialog box.

1. **Access the textbook documents.**

Double-click to open the My Computer window.

Open the 3½ Floppy (A:) window. A window listing the documents to be used with the text should now appear (Figure 2.6).

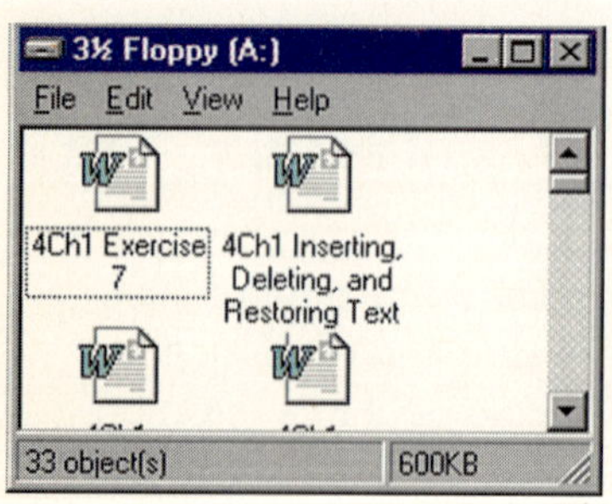

Figure 2.6
The window showing the textbook documents found on drive A.

TIMELY TIP

If you inadvertently drag the pointer as you are holding down (CTRL), you will be executing a Copy command. After the Copy command is executed, one or more icons will appear on the screen labeled Copy of Document, with Document as the name of the document or folder that you inadvertently copied. To get rid of this, click the offending icon and press (DEL). A Confirm File Delete dialog box appears (Figure 2.5). Click the Yes button.

2. **Resize the window so that five icons fit on each row.**

Place the pointer on the size grip, and drag down and to the left until the window is the correct size (Figure 2.7).

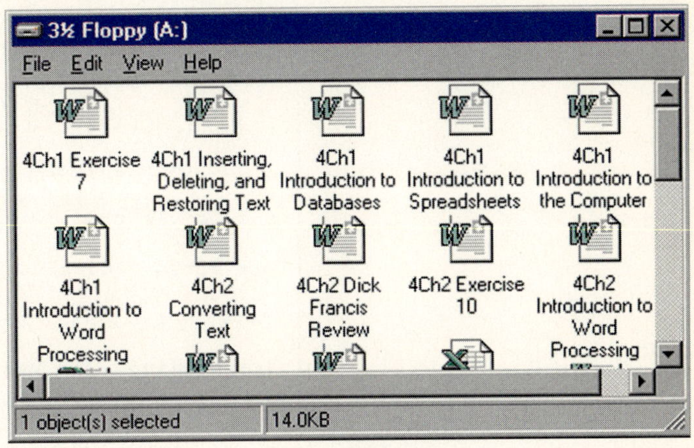

Figure 2.7
The drive A window resized to display five documents across a row.

3. **Open an Excel associated document.**

4Ch3 Exercise 1 Double-click to start Excel and load this document. You should now see the Excel screen shown in Figure 2.8.

Click the Close button on the Excel title bar to return to the window containing the textbook files.

4. **Open a Word associated document.**

4Ch1 Introduction to Word Processing Double-click to start Word and load this document. You should now see the Word screen shown in Figure 2.9.

Click the Close button on the Excel title bar to return to the window containing the textbook files.

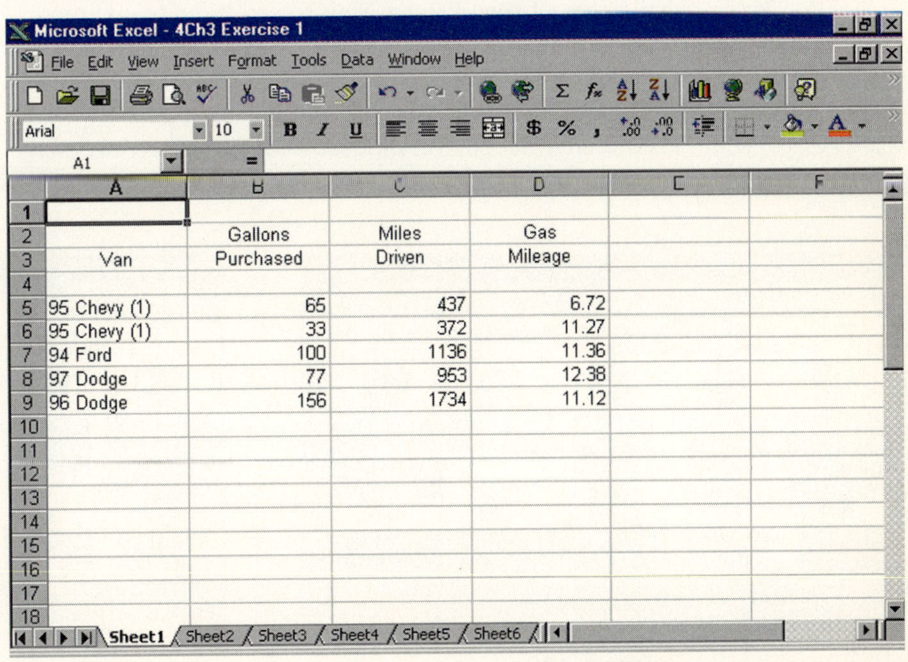

Figure 2.8
The associated *4Ch3 Exercise 1* document displayed using Excel.

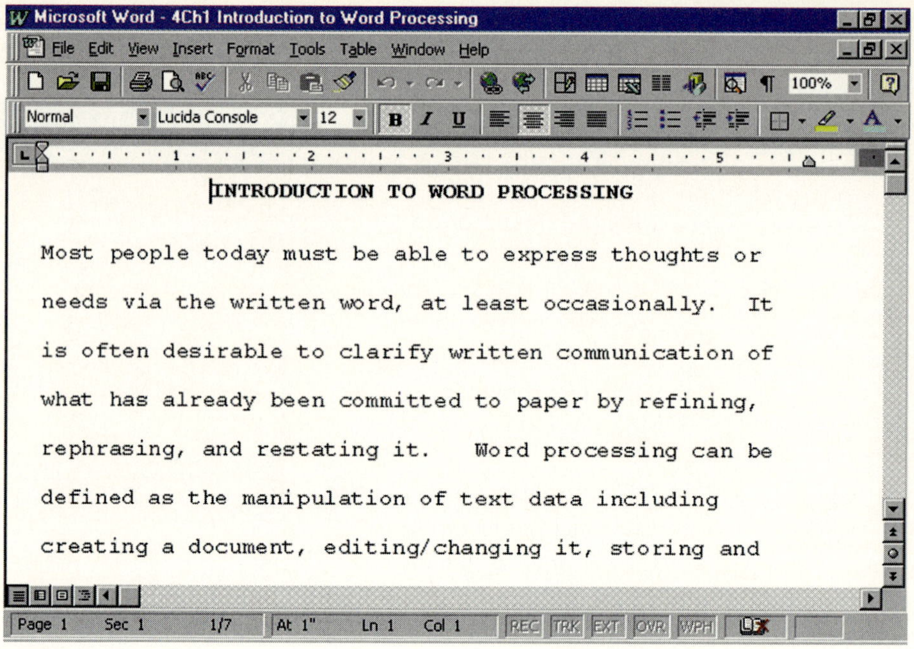

Figure 2.9
The associated *4Ch1 Introduction to Word Processing* document displayed using Microsoft Word.

5. **Select two rows of adjacent documents.**

Click	Click the first document icon in any row.
SHIFT	Hold down SHIFT.
Click	Click the last file in the next row. All the document icons in the two rows should appear in blue, indicating that they have been selected. Your screen should look something like Figure 2.10 (the objects you select may be different).
Click	Click anywhere in the window to deselect the document icons.

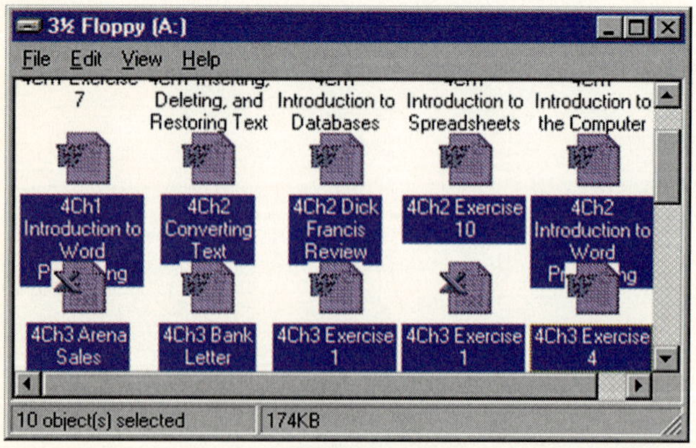

Figure 2.10
Two rows of selected document icons.

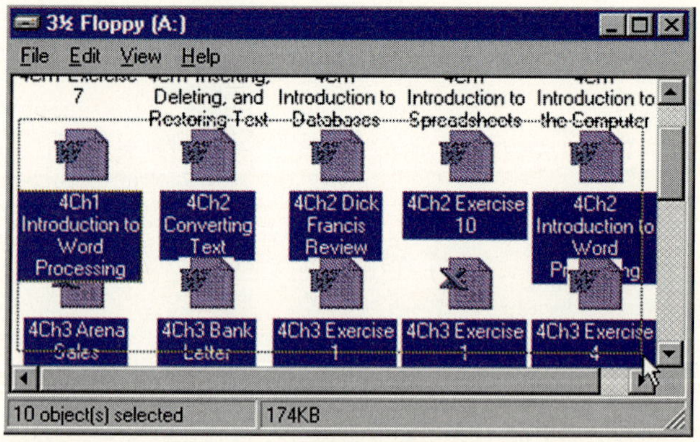

Figure 2.11
The selection rectangle includes objects selected in a drag operation.

6. Use a drag operation to include the same files in a selection.

Click and drag — Click to the left and just above the document icon in any row. Drag until the pointer is below and to the right of the last icon in the next row. Both rows of document icons should be included in the selection, as indicated by the selection rectangle (Figure 2.11). When you release the left mouse button, the objects should appear like those shown in Figure 2.12.

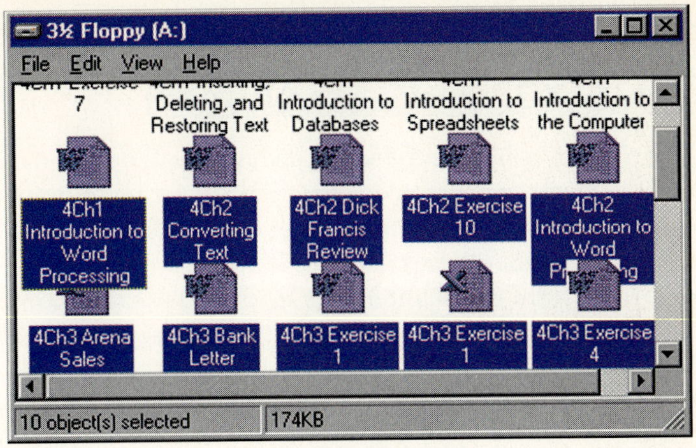

Figure 2.12
The two rows of selected objects.

Click — Click any unused area of the window to cancel the selection.

7. Select every other document icon in the first row.

Click — Click the first document icon in any row.

(CTRL) — Hold down (CTRL).

Click — Click every other document icon to include them in the selection. Your screen should now appear like that shown in Figure 2.13.

Click — Click anywhere in the window to cancel the selection.

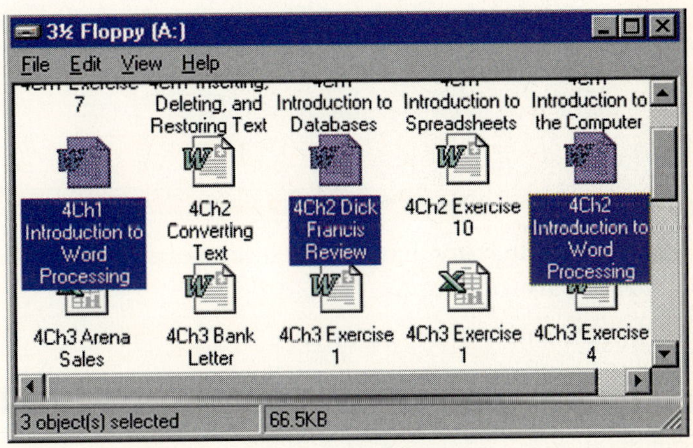

Figure 2.13
Every other object selected in a row.

Reinforcing the Exercise

1. Folders can contain documents or other folders.
2. To select adjacent objects, you click the first object, hold down (SHIFT), and then click the last object.
3. You use (CTRL) in combination with the mouse to select nonadjacent objects.
4. The icon for an associated document includes the icon for the program that was used to create the document.

PERFORMING FILE MAINTENANCE TASKS

The process of file maintenance includes such day-to-day housekeeping tasks as creating new folders; renaming, deleting, moving, or restoring folders and documents; and formatting data disks. These tasks can involve one or more documents.

To perform file maintenance tasks, you use the mouse as the primary input tool. You frequently use the right mouse button to activate the context pop-up menu.

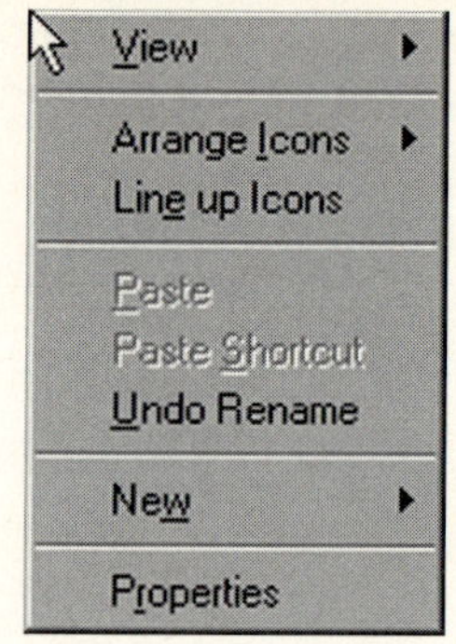

Figure 2.14
The context menu that allows you to start the process of creating a new folder.

Creating a New Folder

The first step in creating a new folder is right-clicking anywhere in the window that will contain the new folder. The context menu shown in Figure 2.14 opens. You then click the New menu option to open the menu shown in Figure 2.15. When you click the Folder option, a selected (blue) folder icon now appears on-screen (Figure 2.16). The default folder name, New Folder, is highlighted so you can immediately enter a new folder name. That folder is now ready to be used for storing any type of file. (Don't worry about the New Folder icon appearing to cover up other folder icons; if you were to leave this window and then come back to it later, the New Folder icon would appear at the bottom.)

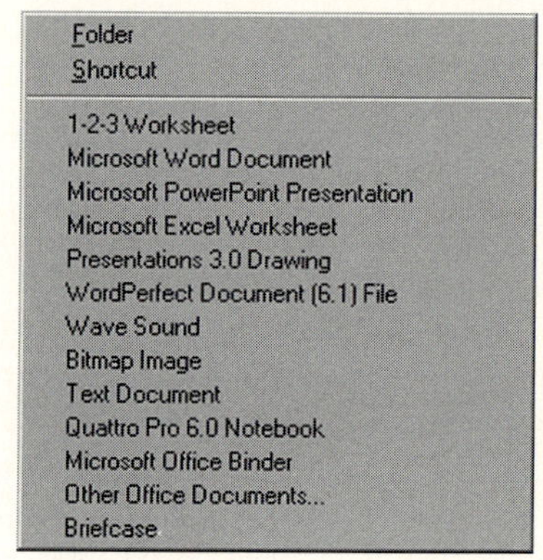

Figure 2.15
The New menu opens when you choose Folder from the context menu.

Hands-On Exercise: Creating a New Folder

Make certain that you have a data disk in drive A. Using the My Computer window, activate drive A.

1. Create a new folder on drive A.

Right-click — Open the context menu by clicking any unused area on the drive A window (Figure 2.14).

New ▶ — Open the New submenu (Figure 2.15). Select the Folder option.

Folder — A new folder now appears with the name New Folder (Figure 2.16). The name is highlighted, indicating you can begin typing a new folder name.

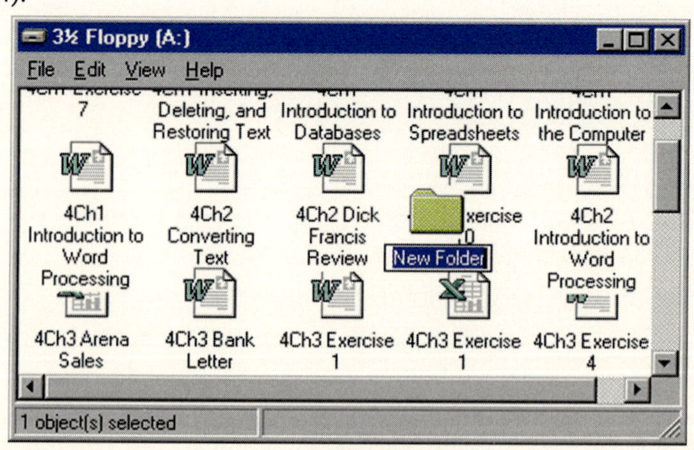

Figure 2.16
The newly inserted folder, ready for you to enter a folder name.

Type: **Temporary Folder** — Double-click the folder name to make certain that the folder has been created. It should be empty, like that shown in Figure 2.17.

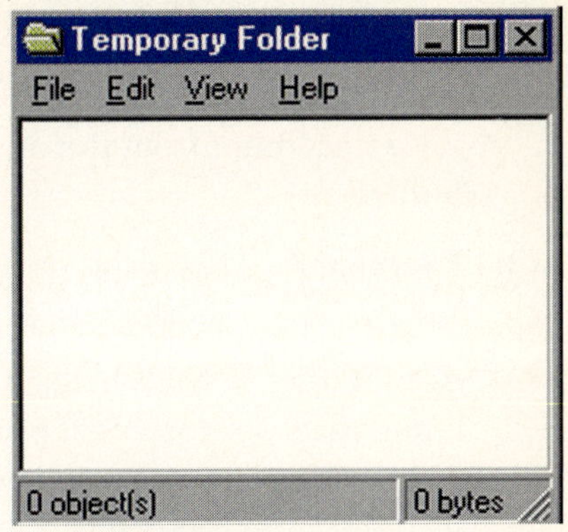

Figure 2.17
The newly created, empty Temporary Folder window displayed.

Reinforcing the Exercise

1. You open a context menu before creating a new folder.
2. The New, Folder command sequence creates a folder with the default name New Folder.
3. You have to enter a name for the created folder, otherwise the default name will be used.

Copying a Document or Folder

The easiest way to copy a document or folder is to select the desired object and then drag it to the desired location.

Occasionally you will need to make copies of important documents stored in a folder on the fixed disk and send them to a disk in drive A. A copy of one or more files saved to disk is called a **backup.** If you later destroy an important document, you can recreate it by copying the backup copy of the document and storing it in the desired folder; this process is called **recovery.**

Once you have selected documents that you wish to copy to a disk, continue to hold down SHIFT or CTRL as you right-click to open the context menu. Select the Send To option to open the menu like that in Figure 2.18. Then select the 3½ Floppy (A) option. The documents are now copied to the disk. Be sure to place the disk with the copied files in a safe place for later use.

If you ever need the backup to recover an important document, use My Computer to open the drive A window, which contains the backup, and the fixed disk window, which contains the folder you want to copy the files to. Use a drag operation to copy the desired documents from the disk to the desired folder on the fixed disk.

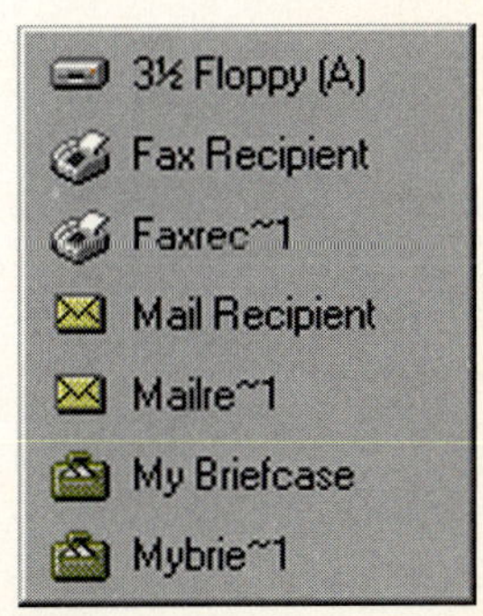

Figure 2.18
The Send To menu.

Hands-On Exercise: Copying a Document

1. **Copy a document from the drive A window to the Temporary Folder Window.**

4Ch1 Exercise 7 — Click this document to select it. It should now appear in blue.

CTRL + Click and drag — While holding down the CTRL key, click and drag the document from the drive A window to the Temporary Folder window. A "phantom" of the icon moves with the operation. When the icon is at the Temporary Folder window, release the mouse button. A text box with a flying folder appears indicating that the document is being copied. When the copy operation is completed, the dialog box disappears, and the document icon appears in both windows. If you don't hold down the CTRL key when you are dragging an item to a location on the same disk, a Move operation will occur instead of a Copy (unless you are selecting a different disk).

2. **Close the Temporary Folder window.**

Click close the Temporary Folder window.

On Your Own

Use the File, New command sequence to add a new folder to the active window.

Reinforcing the Exercise

1. You can copy a document using a drag operation.
2. You can also copy documents using the Send To option of the context menu.
3. One or more documents can be copied at a time.
4. Use the Copy command to execute the backup and recovery processes.

Deleting a Document or Folder

Once you have selected a folder or document, you can delete it by pressing DEL. A Confirm File Delete dialog box appears (Figure 2.19), asking if you really want to delete the indicated object. Click Yes to delete the document or folder.

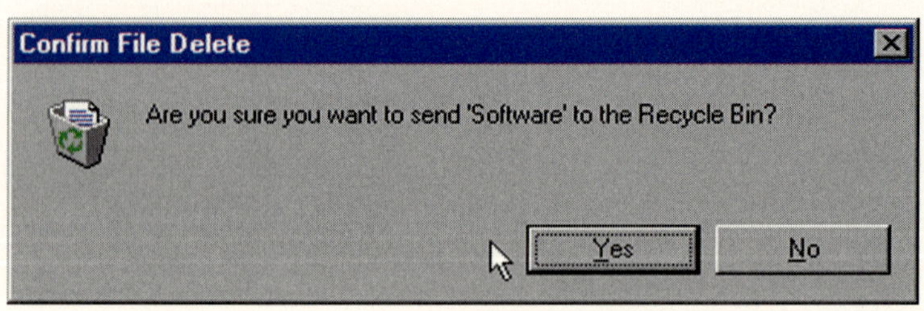

Figure 2.19
The Confirm File Delete dialog box is used by Windows to make certain that you want to delete a document or folder.

Hands-On Exercise: Deleting the Temporary Folder

1. Delete the contents of the Temporary Folder window.

Temporary Folder — Double-click to open the Temporary Folder Window.

4Ch1 Exercise 7 — Click to select the document.

DEL — Press to open the Confirm File Delete dialog box for the 4Ch1 Exercise 7 document (Figure 2.20).

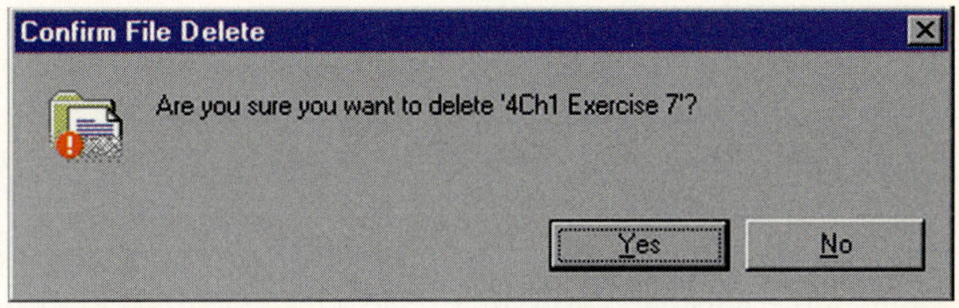

Figure 2.20
The file deletion dialog box for the 4Ch1 Exercise 7 document.

Yes — Click to delete the file. The file icon should no longer be visible in the Temporary Folder window.

X — Click to close the Temporary Folder window.

2. Delete the Temporary Folder.

Temporary Folder — Click this folder icon to select it.

DEL — The Confirm Folder Delete dialog box now appears.

Yes — Click to delete the folder. The text box with a flying folder appears, indicating that the folder is being deleted. When the delete operation is finished, the folder is no longer visible in the drive A window.

TIMELY TIP

You can combine the document delete and folder delete operations into one by deleting a folder without concern for how many files it may hold.

Reinforcing the Exercise

1. Press DEL to delete selected documents or folders.
2. You must confirm that you want to delete the selected documents or folders.
3. When you delete a folder that contains several documents, the documents are deleted as well.

Using the Recycle Bin to Undelete a Document

You will, from time to time, delete a document that you did not want to delete. Don't despair. When Windows deletes a document, it copies it to the **Recycle Bin** so that it can be reconstructed at a later time.

Before you can undelete a document, you must open the window you want to put it in. Then double-click the Recycle Bin on the desktop to see a list of all the recently deleted files (Figure 2.21).

Once you have located the name of the document you want undeleted, you can use a click and drag operation to place it in the desired window. The file is now restored.

TIMELY TIP

Documents saved to disk in Drive A or Drive B, not on the fixed drive, are not copied to the Recycle Bin when they are deleted.

Renaming a Document or Folder

An easy way to rename a document or folder is to right-click that object and then select the Rename command from the context menu. The name of the selected object appears in a rectangle that contains the insertion point (Figure 2.22). When you enter the first character of the new name, the old name is erased. Continue to enter the characters of the new name, and then click any unused area to rename the object.

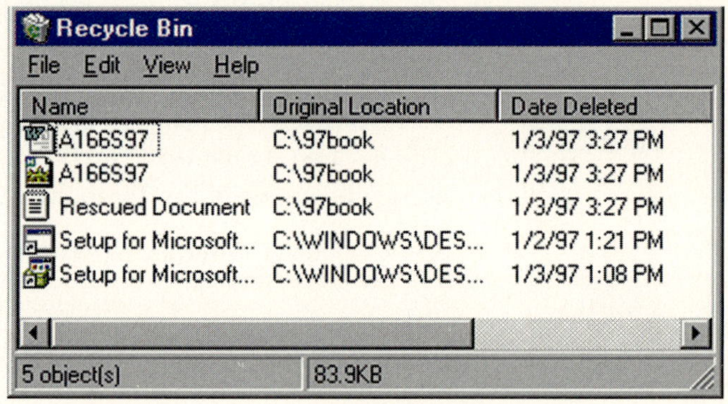

Figure 2.21
The Recycle Bin dialog box lists the deleted documents.

Printing a Document

Windows allows you to print a document that has been associated with a software application. Remember that the icon for an associated document includes the logo of the application to which it is associated. If a document is not associated with an application, the Microsoft flag appears in the icon.

To print an associated document, select the document's icon by clicking it with the mouse, open the File menu from the menu bar, and select the Print command. The associated application is started, the document is loaded, and then it is printed. Once the document has been sent to the printer, you are returned to the window that originally contained that document icon.

Figure 2.22
A document icon that is ready to be renamed.

Verifying the Document to Be Printed

You may not be certain about the contents of a document that you want to print. You can verify a document's contents by selecting

TIMELY TIP

If you are extremely careful, you can also rename a document or folder by positioning the pointer on the name and double-clicking. The name box appears, and you can enter the new object name (Figure 2.22). If you do not have the pointer properly positioned, however, a folder may open or an associated application may start running.

it and then issuing the File, Quick View menu command sequence. The Quick View window opens, displaying the contents of the document (Figure 2.23).

The icons at the top of the Quick View window allow you to perform such tasks as opening the file for editing or increasing or decreasing the size of the font used in the window. You can also view other documents by dragging their icons into the Quick View window.

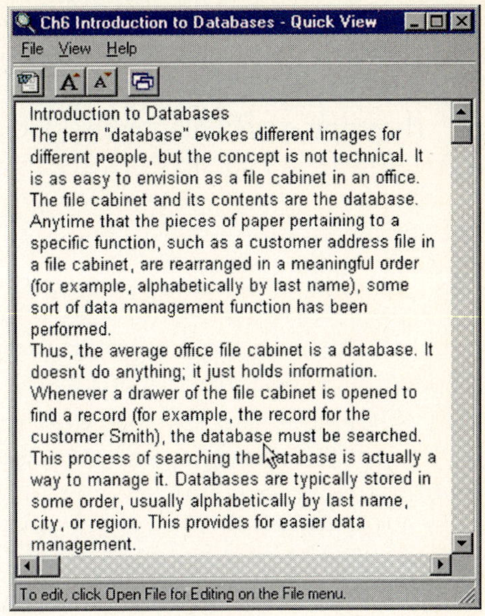

Figure 2.23
The Quick View window allows you to verify the contents of a document before printing it.

FORMATTING A DATA DISK

Before you can use a disk in your computer, it must undergo a process called **formatting.** You use the Format command to initialize the disk so it conforms to a recording format that your computer can use. As it executes, the Format command analyzes the entire disk for defective sectors, initializes the directory (the place on the disk where the document names are kept), sets up space for the file allocation table (which keeps track of the storage areas the document uses), and records the boot program in the boot record. (The boot program loads the system files if they are present or indicates that no system files are present if you try to boot with this disk.)

You access the Format command from the My Computer window. First place the disk to be formatted in the appropriate drive (typically drive A). In the My Computer window, right-click the icon for the drive containing the disk to be formatted (drive A). Then select the Format command to open the Format dialog box shown in Figure 2.24. Make certain that the appropriate disk type is displayed in the Capacity list box. The Format type box provides three basic methods of formatting a disk (Table 2.1).

The first two options listed in Table 2.1 are used by most people for preparing disks for use. The third option is typically irrelevant for creating data disks because there is no need to start the computer with a data disk (it boots from the fixed disk). Besides, the system files take up almost 400,000 bytes of disk space.

TIMELY TIP

Most computer supply stores sell unformatted and preformatted disks. The preformatted disks typically sell for slightly more than unformatted diskettes, but they can save you the aggravation of sending each disk through the formatting process.

The Other options box in the Format dialog box provides three options. The Label option lets you specify a label for the disk. Many students place their names here.

The Copy system files option does the same thing as the Copy system files option discussed in Table 2.1.

The Display summary when finished option is selected by default. This option tells the computer to display a report summary (Figure 2.25).

Once formatting is complete, the system issues a report about the disk in a Format Results dialog box (Figure 2.25). It displays data about the size of the disk and the size of allocation units (sectors). It also displays the volume serial number, which is automatically recorded by Windows and used to identify that specific disk.

During the initial formatting process for a disk, discovery of any defective sectors in a track results in the entire track's being marked as reserved and unavailable for use. This prevents any sectors in the reserved track from being allocated to a data file. Windows reports the total amount of defective space with a screen message (such as "4608 bytes in bad sectors") and subtracts this amount from the total bytes available on the disk (Figure 2.25).

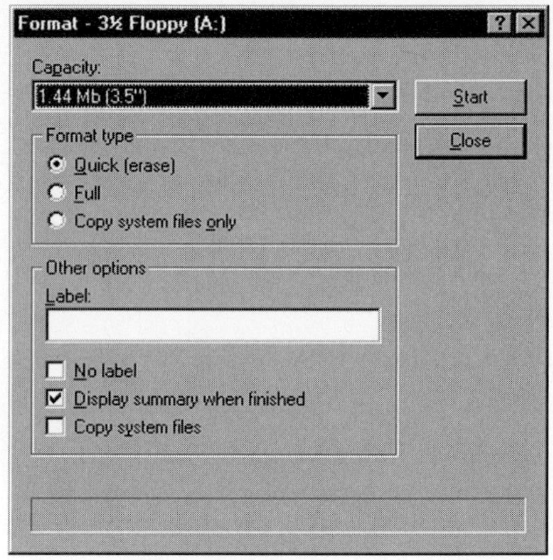

Figure 2.24
The Format dialog box controls how a disk is formatted.

TIMELY TIP

Windows is so careful when it is formatting a disk that it is sometimes too conservative when marking bad sectors. If you format a disk and are informed that it contains bad sectors, try formatting again; on the next try, the sectors may be all right after all.

Table 2.1 Format Types

Option	Task Performed
Quick (erase)	Formats the disk by erasing the files that are present without scanning for bad areas on the disk. It speeds up the formatting process. This option can only be used on disks that have previously been formatted.
Full	Does a complete format of the disk by checking for and marking any bad areas on the disk so that they will not be used later. This option must be used when a disk is formatted for the first time.
Copy system files only	Adds the system files to the disk without formatting so that the disk can be used to start the computer. A disk formatted by this option must be blank.

After you have formatted the disk, click the Close button to return to the Format dialog box. If there are no more disks to be formatted, click the Format dialog box's Close button to return to the My Computer window.

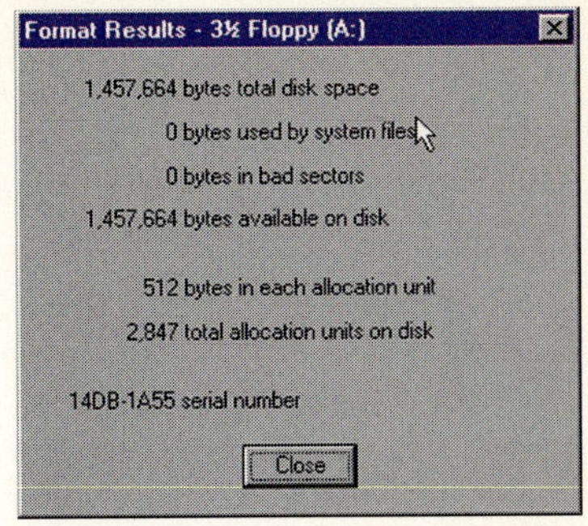

Figure 2.25
The Format Results dialog box showing summary information for a disk that has just been formatted.

USING THE PRINT MANAGER

Printing for all Windows applications is controlled by the **Print Manager.** This means any changes in the printer setup that you make at one location in Windows will affect all Windows application programs. This section introduces you to the Print Manager by showing you how to change the default printer and manipulate the print queue.

Changing the Default Printer

A computer may be connected to more than one printer. The default printer is the one that will print all documents unless Windows is informed otherwise.

On Your Own

Many of the commands covered in this chapter can also be invoked by using the **Explorer** feature of Windows 95 (Figure 2.26). Start Explorer by pointing to the Start button, right-clicking, and selecting the Explore option from the context menu. The Explorer window opens (Figure 2.26). This window has two sections, or panes: the All Folders pane and the Contents pane. These panes display the hierarchy of folders and documents stored on various computer resources. This hierarchy is similar to a tree, with folders and documents branching off from other folders.

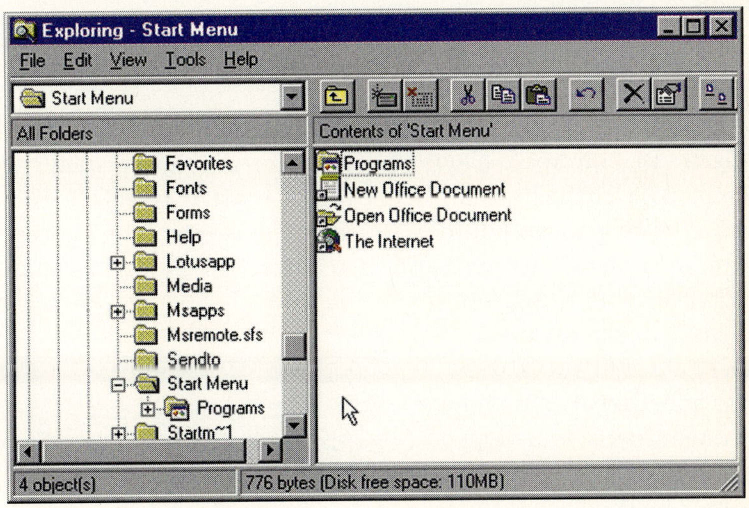

Figure 2.26
The Explorer window

With the Explorer window open, try the following tasks:

- In the All Folders pane, click on an **Expand button** (a plus (+) sign to the left of a folder icon).
- Click on a **Collapse button** (a minus (–) sign to the left of a folder icon).
- In the Contents pane, open a context menu.
- Create a new folder. Name it.
- Copy a document to the new folder.
- Rename the folder.
- Delete the new folder.
- Close Explorer.

To select the default printer, you first enter the command sequence Start, Settings, Printers. In the Printers window that appears (Figure 2.27), click the desired printer. Then issue the command sequence File, Set As Default. The printer you have chosen will be used by all Windows application programs in this and future Windows sessions, until you change the default again. All printing occurs in background mode, which means you can do other tasks while the printing process proceeds.

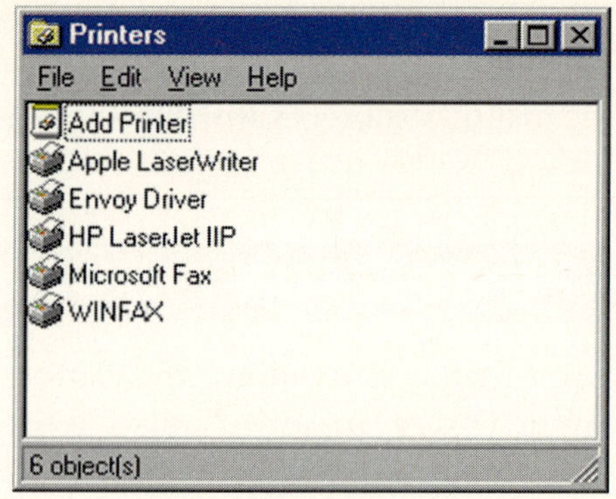

Figure 2.27
The Printers window allows you to select the default printer.

Checking Printer Status and Managing the Print Queue

The Print Manager icon appears at the bottom of the screen in the status bar when any print operations are being performed. This indicates that the Print Manager is running in **background mode,** printing any jobs that you have sent to the printer. If something goes wrong during a print run (for instance, you receive a message indicating that the printer is not working), a red question mark becomes part of the Print Manager icon. Double-click the icon to display the Print Manager window. For example, the Print Manager window shown in Figure 2.28 indicates that an Apple LaserWriter has paused. It also displays a list of documents waiting to be printed, called the **print queue.**

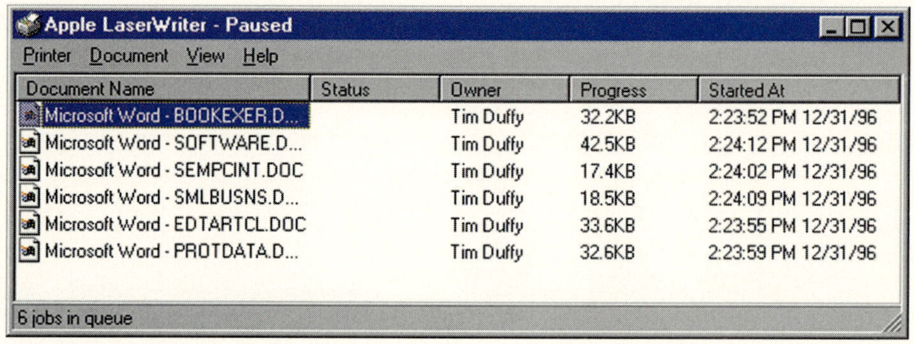

Figure 2.28
The Print Manager window for the Apple LaserWriter with several files ready for printing.

To delete a document from the print queue, click the appropriate name in the Document Name list, and then enter the command sequence Document, Cancel Printing. You can also change the position of a document in the print queue by clicking the document name and dragging it to a new location. Figure 2.29 shows that the EDTARTCL and PROTDATA documents have been moved in front of the SOFTWARE document. You cannot move a document in front of a document currently being printed.

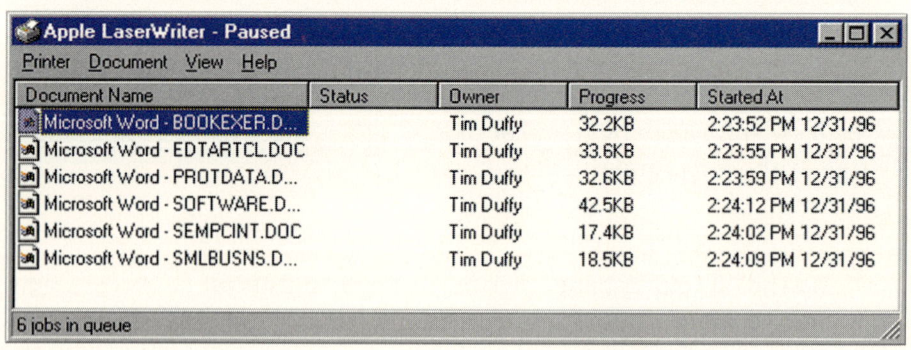

Figure 2.29
The order of the files in the print queue has been changed by dragging.

SESSION REVIEW

Windows 95 provides a file maintenance system that allows you to manipulate items you have saved to disk.

Windows uses a folder metaphor to describe its file maintenance system. Documents (files) are stored in folders. Folders can be nested in one another; that is, a folder can have several different levels of folders. A folder can contain such things as part of the operating system, a workbook, and a word processing document.

Before you can work with documents and folders, you must select them. You select a single document or folder by clicking the desired object. To select multiple adjacent objects, you drag the pointer over the desired objects, or hold down SHIFT and then click the first and last objects. Select multiple nonadjacent objects by holding down CTRL and clicking the desired objects.

When you double-click an associated file, the application program that was used to create that object automatically starts.

File maintenance tasks include creating new folders, renaming existing objects, copying objects from one location to another, deleting an object from disk, or restoring an object using the Recycle Bin.

Windows provides several methods for formatting a disk. Any disk must be formatted at least once. Two of the formatting methods are commonly used for preparing data disks for use.

The Explorer feature of Windows provides much of the same information as the My Computer window, but the Explorer window presents two panes of data. The leftmost pane, labeled All Folders, shows the hierarchy of the folders using a tree structure. To expand the tree, you click a button with a plus sign (+), called an Expand button, which appears to the left of a folder name. To reduce the tree, you click a button with a minus sign (−), called a Collapse button. The rightmost pane in the Explorer window, labeled Contents, shows the contents of the selected folder or drive.

The Print Manager controls how files are printed. All print operations using Windows go through the Print Manager. You can use the Print Manager to cancel print operations that have already been started by a Windows application program.

KEY TERMS AND CONCEPTS

SESSION QUIZ

Multiple Choice

1. Which of the following do you use to select multiple adjacent objects?
   a. SHIFT
   b. CTRL
   c. a drag operation
   d. all of the above
2. Which of the following statements about Explorer is/are false?
   a. It allows you to delete documents.
   b. It allows you to control which types of documents and folders are listed.
   c. It lists only one folder or disk device at a time.
   d. It allows you to specify more than one object.
3. Which of the following statements is false regarding folders and the My Computer window?
   a. You can rename a folder.
   b. You can delete a folder.
   c. You can create a folder.
   d. You can print a document.
   e. None of the above.
4. Which of the following options of the Format dialog box cannot be used on a disk?
   a. Label
   b. Copy system files
   c. Quick (erase)
   d. Copy directory
5. How do you alter the position of a document in the Print Manager print queue?
   a. Select the Priority command and select the next document.
   b. Select the Rush command from the Options menu.
   c. Click the desired document and drag it to the new location in the print queue.
   d. None of the above.

True/False

6. The drive icons allow you to control which folders and files are displayed using Explorer.
7. When specifying multiple objects for an operation, you can specify only adjacent object names.
8. You can restore deleted files using the Recycle Bin.
9. Before you can open an associated document, you must start the related application program.
10. The Print Manager controls the printing of any Windows application program.

SESSION REVIEW EXERCISES

1. Define the following terms:
   a. Print Manager
   b. print queue
   c. Recycle Bin
   d. associated file
2. When you double-click a(n) ______________ document, the application program automatically starts, and then the document opens.
3. The ______________ command is used to prepare a disk for use by the computer.
4. Folders are created using the ______________ command of the context menu.
5. Folders are erased by pressing the ______________ key.
6. Folders and documents can be renamed using the ______________ command from the context menu.
7. The File ______________ command can only be used with associated documents.
8. The Recycle Bin lets you restore a document from the fixed disk but does not let you restore a file that was erased from a ______________ .
9. The ______________ pane of the Explorer contains a list of the folders and documents in the selected drive or folder.
10. In the Explorer Window, a folder icon with a ______________ sign has no branch folders.
11. You must hold down the ______________ key when you are using the mouse to select multiple nonadjacent documents or folders.
12. The process of copying files to a disk to protect the original files is called ______________ .
13. You can select multiple adjacent documents by holding down the ______________ key.
14. You can also select multiple adjacent documents by using a ______________ operation.
15. A selected document or folder appears ______________ in a different color.
16. To see the contents of a document before printing, you must use the ______________ ______________ command.
17. A document in the Recycle Bin can be restored by ______________ it to its original window.
18. A document name can contain up to ______________ characters.
19. The process of fixing a damaged or deleted file by copying a file to the fixed disk is called ______________ .
20. You can delete a ______________ or document by using DEL.

COMPUTER EXERCISES

1. Use the Format command to format any disks that you will be using this school term. Be sure to format them as data disks. You do not want the system files on any of these disks.
2. Create the folder structure shown in Figure 2.30. This exercise reinforces the folder concepts introduced in this chapter. It requires that you have the student data disk used with this text in drive A.

   After you have built the new folders, start Explorer. Expand all of the folders. Your Explorer window should look like that shown in Figure 2.31. Once you complete this exercise, delete all folders.

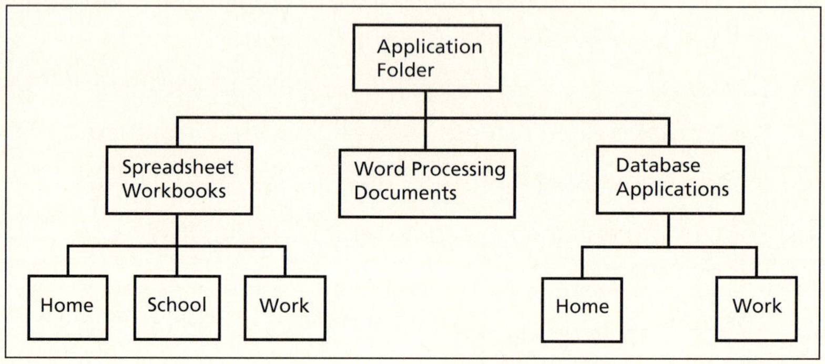

Figure 2.30
The hierarchy of the folder structure to be created.

3. This exercise reinforces the use of the New and Copy commands. It requires you to open the disk area that contains your textbook-related documents.
   a. Create a new folder and name it Temporary Storage Area.
   b. Copy the following documents to it: 4Ch1 Introduction to Spreadsheets, 4Ch1 Introduction to the Computer, and 4Ch1 Introduction to Databases.
   c. Open the Temporary Storage Area folder to verify that the documents were copied correctly.
   d. Close the Temporary Storage Area folder.
   e. Delete the Temporary Storage Area folder.
4. Double-click the 4Ch1 Introduction to Databases associated document. The document should be loaded automatically by Word. Click the Close button of the Word window to return to the desktop.
5. Select the 4Ch1 Introduction to Spreadsheets document. Issue a File, Quick View command sequence. Your screen should now appear like that shown in Figure 2.32.
   a. Use the scroll bar to examine the document.
   b. Click the Open file for editing button. Word should now be started, and the document opened.
   c. Click the Close button of the Word window to return to the desktop.

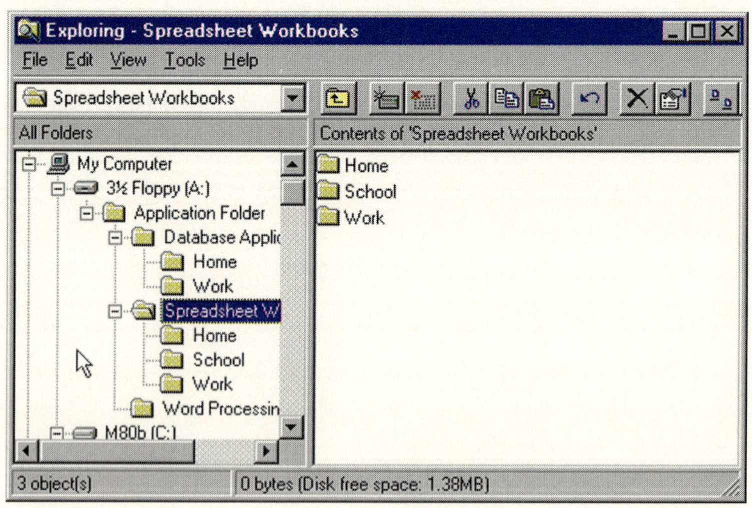

Figure 2.31
The newly created folders shown in expanded format by using the Explorer window.

6. Select the 4Ch1 Introduction to Databases document.
   a. Issue the File, Print command sequence.
   b. The document should begin printing.
   c. After the document is printed, you should be returned to the desktop.
   d. If the printer icon is visible in the lower-right corner of your screen, double-click it to invoke the Print Manager. Examine the window and the status of the print process.
   e. Click the Close button of the Print Manager window to return to the desktop.
7. Use the Explorer feature of Windows to examine the device and/or folder used for storing your textbook documents.
8. Experiment with selecting multiple documents by using the mouse.
   a. Select adjacent documents by using a drag operation.
   b. Select adjacent documents by using (SHIFT).
   c. Select nonadjacent documents by using (CTRL).
9. Activate the Recyle Bin to see if there are any documents that you can restore. If possible, restore one of the documents that you have erased previously (remember, if your original files resided on drive A, they cannot be restored using the Recycle Bin).
10. Use the Start, Printers Setting command sequence to see if there are any other printers that you can use with your Windows installation. Close the window when you are finished.

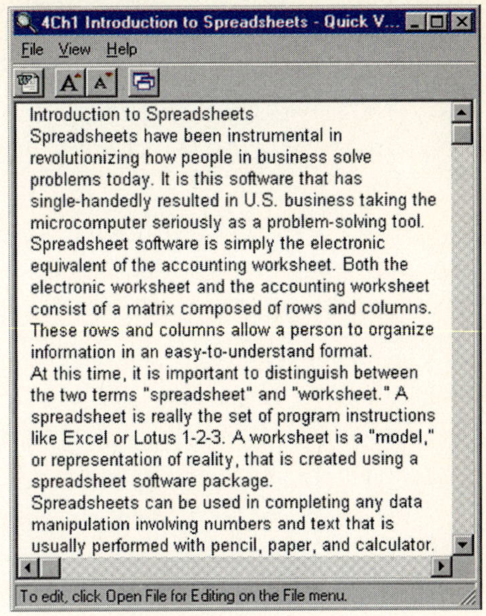

Figure 2.32
The 4Ch1 Introduction to Spreadsheets document displayed in the Quick View window.

Notes

Notes

Notes

Notes

Notes

Notes

Notes

OPERATIONS REFERENCE

BUTTON OR ICON	OPERATION	EXPLANATION
	Starting Windows 95	Turn on your computer.
	Logging onto a network system	In the opening box, enter your user name, press TAB, and enter your password.
	Opening the Start menu	Click the Start button on the taskbar.
	Closing the Start menu	Click any unused area of the desktop.
	Shutting down Windows	Choose Shut Down from the Start menu. The *Shut down the computer?* option is the default. Click Yes.
	Shutting down Windows (on a network system)	Choose Shut Down from the Start menu, click the *Close all programs and log on as a different user* option, and then click Yes.
	Launching (running) a program	Select Programs from the Start menu and then choose the desired program.
	Switching between running programs	Click the button on the taskbar that represents the desired program.
	Closing (shutting down) a program	Click the program's Close button, or choose Close (or Exit) from the File menu.
	Moving a window	Click the window's title bar and drag the window to the new location.
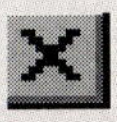	Closing a window	Click the window's Close button.
	Resizing a window	Drag the size grip in the lower-right corner of the window, or drag any border or corner.
	Minimizing a window	Click the window's Minimize button.
	Maximizing a window	Click the window's Maximize button.

BUTTON OR ICON	OPERATION	EXPLANATION
	Restoring a window to its premaximized size	Click the window's Restore button. This button replaces the Maximize button on a maximized window.
	Moving through a screen one line at a time	Click the up or down arrow in the scroll bar.
	Moving quickly through a screen	Drag the scroll box.
	Selecting an object	Click the object once.
	Deselecting an object	Click any unused area of the desktop.
	Selecting multiple adjacent objects	Click the first object and drag to the last object until a rectangle encloses all the desired objects.
	Selecting multiple nonadjacent objects	Press CTRL as you click the desired objects.
	Displaying an object's context menu	Right-click the object. If the object is a window, right-click its title bar.
	Moving an object	Click the object and drag it to the new location.
	Arranging objects	From the desktop or the My Computer window, right-click any blank area and then choose Arrange Icons from the context menu.
	Dragging an object	Hold down the left mouse button while moving the mouse, and release the mouse button to drop the object.
	Creating a folder	Right-click any unused area of the desktop to open a context menu, choose New, and then choose Folder.
	Creating a backup copy of folders or documents	Place a disk in drive A. Select the folders or documents in the appropriate drive window (accessed via My Computer), hold down CTRL as you right-click to open a context menu, and then choose the 3½ Floppy (A:) option.
	Copying a folder or document to another window	Double-click the My Computer icon to open the My Computer window, and then open the window to receive the copy. Click the folder or document icon, and then hold down CTRL while you drag the folder to the other window.

BUTTON OR ICON	OPERATION	EXPLANATION
	Deleting a folder or document	Click the folder or document icon in the My Computer window and then press DEL.
	Retrieving a deleted folder or document	Click the Recycle Bin icon and then click and drag the desired folder or document to the window where you would like it to be located.
	Renaming a folder or document	Right-click the folder or document icon in the My Computer window and choose Rename from the context menu.
	Examining the contents of a disk	Double-click the My Computer icon and double-click the icon from the desired disk.
	Examining the contents of a folder	Double-click the icon for the desired folder in the My Computer window.
	Formatting a disk	Place the disk in the appropriate drive, open the My Computer window, and click Format on the menu bar.
	Printing a document	Click the icon for the document in the My Computer window and then issue the File, Print command sequence.
	Viewing a document	Click the icon for the document in the My Computer window and then issue the File, Quick View command sequence.
	Checking the status of a print job in the Print Manager window	Double-click the Print Manager icon in the status bar of the document waiting to be printed.
	Deleting a document from the print queue	Click the document name in the Print Manager window and issue the Document, Cancel command sequence.
	Changing the status of a document in the print queue	Click the document name and drag it to the desired location in the print queue.

GLOSSARY

active window The window that appears on top when multiple windows are open on the desktop. Any commands you issue or text you enter affects only the active window.

associated document A document that has been saved to disk by a specific software application and is represented in a folder by an icon with an application logo on it. When you select an associated document, the application that was used to create that document is started and the document is loaded.

background mode The Print Manager can run printing jobs as you complete other tasks. During background mode, the Print Manager icon appears in the status bar, and if something goes wrong during a print job, a red question mark becomes part of the Print Manager icon.

backup A copy of one or more files saved to disk.

border The edge of a window. When you position the pointer on the border, the pointer changes to a double-headed arrow, which allows you to resize the window.

click To quickly press and release the left mouse button; done to select an object.

clipboard An area in memory used to store data temporarily during a cut, paste, or copy operation. The clipboard can store data only for one Cut or Copy command; the data in the clipboard is destroyed and replaced when a subsequent Cut or Copy command is issued.

Close button The rightmost button on the title bar used to close a window or application.

Collapse button In the All Folders pane of Explorer, you click this button to close a folder and hide its contents.

command sequence A series of menu selections. For example, to issue the File, Open command sequence, you choose File from the menu bar and then choose Open from the File menu.

control Object within a dialog box, such as a text box, list box, check box, or command button.

control-menu button Located at the far left end of a window's title bar, this button is a throwback to older versions of Windows and is now rarely used.

deselect To reverse the action of selecting an object by clicking anywhere outside the selected object.

desktop An on-screen workspace on which you can perform a variety of tasks by clicking buttons or icons that represent applications, commands, or files.

dialog box A type of window that prompts you for information needed to carry out a command. A dialog box opens when you select a menu option that has an ellipsis after its name or when you click certain buttons.

disk operating system (DOS) A set of programs that allows you to interact with the computer.

document Represents stored data that can be processed by an application program or by the computer itself.

double-click To press and release the left mouse button twice in rapid succession.

drag To press and hold the left mouse button while moving the mouse; done to select multiple lines or to move an object to another location.

Expand button In the All Folders pane of Explorer, you click this button to open a folder and display its contents.

Explorer A feature of Windows 95 that displays the hierarchy of folders and documents stored on various computer resources. Using Explorer, you can execute many file maintenance commands.

file Computer term, rather than a Windows-related term, for a document.

file maintenance The process of interacting with objects that you have saved to disk.

folder In Windows' file maintenance system, the storage place for documents or other folders.

format The process of initializing a disk so it conforms to a recording format that your computer can use. The formatting process includes analyzing the disk for defective sectors, initializing the directory, setting up space for the allocation table, and recording the boot program.

graphic user interface (GUI) A software program that allows you to communicate with your computer by using a pointing device called a mouse. This tool for executing commands is quicker than a text-based environment, in which you execute commands by entering keystrokes.

Help feature A Windows feature that provides information on all desktop objects.

icon A graphic representation of an object on the desktop.

inactive window Any window that appears beneath the active window. You can click anywhere on an inactive window to make it the active window.

Maximize button Click this button to enlarge a window so it fills the entire screen.

menu bar Located under the title bar in a window, the menu bar contains the names of menus you can open to access commands. Windows is consistent in how menus are arranged from application to application, making it easy to learn various Windows applications.

Minimize button Click this button to take the window off the desktop and place a button for it on the taskbar.

mouse A pointing device used in conjunction with a graphic user interface to execute commands quickly and easily.

multitasking Windows capability to run multiple applications at one time.

object Any item that appears on the desktop, such as a document, a field in a database, or a button on a toolbar.

operating system A complex set of computer instructions that comes between you and your computer. It accepts a command from the user, evaluates that command, and then executes it.

point To move the mouse so that the pointer rests on an object.

Print Manager Controls all printing operations for Windows.

print queue A list of documents waiting to be printed displayed in the Print Manager window.

property Controls how an object behaves and operates in a Windows environment. An object can have several properties, and you control the properties of an object by entering values in a properties sheet.

pull-down menu A menu opened from the menu bar.

recovery The process of recreating a lost or damaged document by copying the backup copy.

Recycle Bin A storage area for deleted documents. You can recover a document from the Recycle Bin and put it back in a folder so you can work on it.

resize a window Performed by using a drag operation on the window border.

Restore button Replaces the Maximize button on a window that you have maximized. Click this button to return a window to the size it was before you clicked the Maximize button.

right-click To press the right mouse button; done to open a context menu.

ScreenTip A text box that appears when you click the What's This button and then click an object. The ScreenTip provides more detailed information on the function of the object than the ToolTip.

scroll bar Located on the right border of a window and contains a scroll box and up and down arrow buttons. Click the up or down arrow button to move up or down the screen one line at a time.

scroll box Part of the scroll bar. You can drag the scroll box up or down to move quickly from one part of a document to another. The position of the scroll box indicates the location of the cursor in the displayed text.

select adjacent objects Accomplished in two ways: You can click the first object, hold down (SHIFT), and then click the last object; all objects between the two clicked objects are included in the selection. You can also use a drag operation: click the first object and drag the pointer to include the last object.

select nonadjacent objects Hold down (CTRL) as you click the objects.

shortcut command A command entered from the keyboard.

size grip An icon located in the lower-right corner of a window. When you position the pointer on a size grip, the pointer changes to a double-headed arrow. You can then resize the window by using a drag operation.

status bar Located at the bottom of the window, the status bar provides information on an object from the desktop that you select.

taskbar The gray bar that always appears at the bottom of the Windows desktop and contains the Start button and application buttons representing currently open applications or windows.

title bar Colored bar at the top of a window that contains the name of the open application and four buttons you can use to control the window: the control-menu, Minimize, Maximize (or Restore), and Close buttons.

ToolTip A small text box that appears when you position the pointer on an object and let it rest there a while. The ToolTip provides information on the function of the object.

WYSIWYG Stands for "what you see is what you get" and refers to the Windows method of displaying text on-screen exactly as it will print to paper.

INDEX